CROSS *for baby* STITCH *and nursery* GIFTS

CROSS
for baby
STITCH
and nursery
GIFTS

SANDRA HARDY

Photographs by Shona Wood

NEW HOLLAND

First published in 1999 by
New Holland Publishers (UK) Ltd
London • Cape Town • Sydney • Singapore

24 Nutford Place
London W1H 6DQ
United Kingdom

80 McKenzie Street
Cape Town 8001
South Africa

3/2 Aquatic Drive
Frenchs Forest, NSW 2086
Australia

ISBN 1 85368 802 9

Created and produced by Rosemary Wilkinson Publishing,
38 Halton Road, London N1 2EU

Designed by Roger Daniels
Chart artwork by Stephen Dew
Techniques illustrations by Kate Simunek
Additional photographs on pages 22 to 23 by Caroline Arber

Reproduction by PICA Colour Separation, Singapore
Printed and bound in Malaysia by Times Offset (M) Sdn. Bhd.
2 4 6 8 10 9 7 5 3 1

Contents

Introduction

The arrival of a new baby is always such a special event, bringing a wealth of joy and happiness to friends and family.

Hand stitched gifts that have been especially made for the new baby must undeniably be the most treasured ones, both to give and to receive. Often kept for many years after the baby's arrival, they can become family heirlooms for future generations.

This book features a varied selection of stitching projects, designed to appeal to both the new stitcher and the most dedicated. Projects such as the pink and yellow Tulip Blouse will be completed in next-to-no time, while the Cheeky Clowns Number Picture and Teddy Bear Cot Quilt will keep you stitching for many a long hour.

Styles vary enormously too, from the traditional swirling alphabet which decorates the Christening gown, to the bright and comic rabbits which appear on the hand towel or the dinosaurs on the toy bag.

This book also includes specially designed gifts to mark those special occasions in a baby's life, including cards to celebrate his or her arrival and a fairy photograph album to record the Christening or the first birthday.

Eye-catching and decorative wearables for every occasion are in abundance, handmade Butterfly Bootees for that summer pram ride, a Nautical Sun Hat for the first holiday, fashionable denim dungarees for playtime and the prettiest daisy dress and matching pants for that special outing.

Preparing a nursery for the new baby is both pleasurable and exciting, so several ideas are included for co-ordinating furnishings and producing decorative accessories. A stunning repeat daisy motif made into a curtain trim and matched with a buttercup tie back are surrounded by a smiling sheep sheet, an enchanted castle cot blanket, a flower and teddy sampler and lots more.

A range of baby stitching would not be complete without toys to entertain that special little person. A row of boy and girl teddy bears link across the cot or pram, guaranteed to produce a smile and there's a larger teddy bear designed for a slightly older baby or toddler.

Finally, there are suggestions at the end of each project for varying and adapting the designs. Once started in this direction, I am sure you will see more and more possibilities.

So, I hope you enjoy stitching these designs and using them as a starting point for your own ideas for the new baby and the nursery.

Sandra Hardy

Chapter One

For Baby's Wardrobe

Christening Gown and Petticoat

How better to mark that very special occasion in your baby's life than to personalise the Christening gown with beautiful hand stitching. The Victorian style lettering is decorated with swirling flowers and leaves to create these attractive motifs. Additional flowers have been stitched to the sleeve edges and petticoat hem and the design is given in two alternative colourways. Christening gowns are perfect pieces of baby clothing to be passed down through the generations, becoming more and more treasured on their way. The dresses used here were, in fact, everyday dresses made by my Grandmother for my Mother, when she was a baby. They were worn by my daughters for their Christenings, and maybe one day will be used again for their babies.

Finished size of stitching:
initial varying between 6 - 10 cm (2½ - 4 in)
petticoat 9 × 2 cm (3 ½ × ¾ in)

MATERIALS
White waste canvas, 14 count, size 12 × 50 cm (4¾ × 19½ in), sufficient for dress and six sets of flowers on the petticoat

DMC STRANDED COTTON:

for either colourway, 1 skein each of

966 pale fern green

564 pale silver green

827 pale sea blue

775 very pale dusty blue

plus, for apricot colourway, 1 skein each of

352 salmon pink

754 very pale salmon pink

948 creamy pink

plus, for pink colourway, 1 skein each of

818 very pale rose pink

962 deep pink

3326 pale rose pink

Chenille or embroidery needle
Christening gown and petticoat

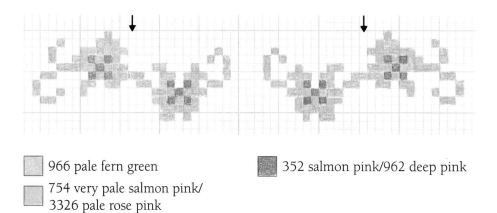

966 pale fern green

754 very pale salmon pink/
3326 pale rose pink

352 salmon pink/962 deep pink

STITCHING INSTRUCTIONS

1 For the dress, attach the waste canvas in the appropriate position on the dress with tacking stitches, following the instructions on page 114. I placed the design at the bottom of the skirt to one side.

2 Use one strand of cotton only and work in cross stitch throughout. Take great care to keep the back of the work as tidy as possible, as any threads beyond the design edges may show through to the right side.

3 Choose the appropriate initial from the alphabet chart on pages 118 to 121 and start stitching the initial first, then complete the background stalks, leaves and flowers. Remove the waste canvas and tacking carefully.

4 For the petticoat stitching, first measure the circumference of the hem and decide how many groups of flowers are to be worked. Mark the centre of each of these before attaching the waste canvas and starting to stitch, following the chart on page 10.

5 Work in the same way to stitch groups of flowers round the sleeve edges of the gown.

ADAPTATIONS AND VARIATIONS

1 These attractive initials can be used to personalise any cot or pram pillowcases, sheets and blankets.

2 If 14 count Aida or 28 count evenweave is used instead of the waste canvas, then these initals would be very suitable for a birth congratulations or first birthday greetings card.

3 Why not stitch the complete name of the baby for a very special picture or name plaque? A border around this could be made from the flower motif used for the petticoat and sleeves.

Butterfly Bootees

What could be nicer for a mother and baby than to receive these hand-made and decoratively stitched bootees as a gift? The fine white linen fabric has been attractively finished with white satin ribbon binding and ties.

Finished size of stitching:
3 × 2.5 cm (1⅛ × 1 in)

Finished size of bootees:
12 cm (4¾ in) length

MATERIALS

White Belfast linen, 32 count, size 21 × 30 cm
  (8.5 × 12 in)
White sewing thread
White satin ribbon, 13 mm (½ in) wide,
  1.5 m (60 in) long

DMC STRANDED COTTON:

1 skein each of

■ 809 pale blue

□ 3823 ivory

▢ 726 pale gold

Tapestry needle, size 26

MAKING THE BOOTEES

1 Trace the pattern pieces from the design given on page 122 and onto paper. Note that all edges have a 0.5 cm (¼ in) seam allowance already added.

2 Pin these pieces onto the linen and cut two of each. Remember to reverse the sole piece, which is for the left foot, in order to cut the opposite for the right foot.

3 Take one of the upper pieces and bring the two short edges together, right sides together. Pin and stitch the seam, taking a 0.5 cm (¼ in) allowance. Repeat with the second upper piece. Trim the seam by oversewing by hand or machine.

4 Pin the lower edge of the upper to the sole, right sides together and taking the usual seam allowance. Ease the rounded edges of the sole to fit the upper but try to avoid any tucks. Stitch the seam and trim as before.

5 Bind the opening with the satin ribbon, starting and finishing at the back of the bootee. Cut the remaining ribbon into two lengths and trim the ends into a V shape. Fold the ribbons in half and attach to the back of the bootee to cover the join in the binding. The bootee is now ready to be stitched.

STITCHING INSTRUCTIONS

1 Mark the centre of the upper front bootee area with a tacking thread, and use this to start stitching the butterfly's body following the chart below.

2 Work both the cross stitching and the backstitching using one strand of cotton.

3 Complete all the cross stitching before working the back stitching. Take care not to jump across the back of the linen with the dark blue thread, from area to area, as this will be visible from the right side.

ADAPTATIONS AND VARIATIONS

1 Pale yellow or blue ribbons could be substituted for the white ones if more colour was wanted on this item.

2 These delicate butterflies are an ideal motif for the dress and pants in the Pink Daisy Layette on page 19. Stitched on with waste canvas, the embroidery will make a really eye-catching outfit for a special occasion.

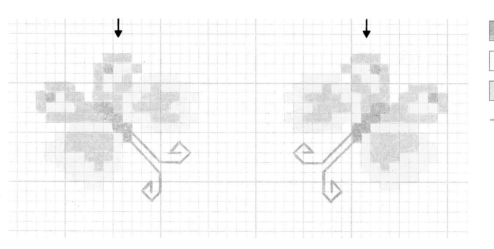

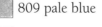

■ 809 pale blue

□ 3823 ivory

□ 726 pale gold

— 809 pale blue

Animal Faces Babygros

A quick and easy project showing two choices of design to transform a plain sleeping suit into something a little special and original. These attractive motifs are embroidered in Flower Threads; a type of soft, matt, non-divisible embroidery yarn designed essentially for relatively fine stitching. Using waste canvas means that you can stitch the motifs on any kind of suit, whether velour, stretch-knit or towelling.

Finished size of stitching:
approximately 9×8 cm (3½×3⅛ in)

MATERIALS
White waste canvas, 14 count, size 12×10 cm
   (4¾×4 in) for each motif

DMC FLOWER THREADS:

for white babygro, 1 skein each of

 2776 pink

2819 palest pink

for blue babygro, 1 skein each of

2798 mid blue

2775 pale blue

Chenille or embroidery needle
Plain white and blue babygros

STITCHING INSTRUCTIONS

1 It is a good idea to use a close machine zig-zag stitch or binding on the cut edges of the waste canvas, so that these do not snag the babygro while the stitching is being worked. Follow the instructions on page 114.

2 Tack the waste canvas over the area to be stitched, taking care not to stretch the fabric of the babygro.

3 Work the cross stitch and back stitch using a single strand of flower thread.

4 Following the chart opposite, work the outlines of the motifs in cross stitch first, then fill in the areas within the outlines. Complete by backstitching the cat's and dog's mouths, and the mouse's whiskers.

5 Remove the tacking stitches from the waste canvas, then pull out the warp (vertical) and weft (horizontal) threads one by one.

ADAPTATIONS AND VARIATIONS

1 Any number of these motifs could be stitched through waste canvas on any item of clothing or bed linen, using a contrast colour thread in two shades.

2 If a larger motif is preferred, a lower count waste canvas could be used, for example an 11 count canvas would give an approximate finished size of 11.5 × 10 cm (4½ × 4 in). For this perhaps a thicker thread should be used to give extra definition to the design: three strands of cotton, or coton à broder would be suitable.

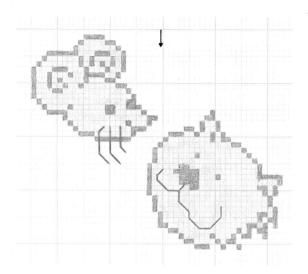

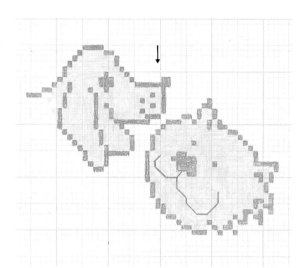

2776 pink

2819 palest pink

— 2776 pink

2798 mid blue

2775 pale blue

— 2798 mid blue

Pink Daisy Layette

Preparing for the arrival of a new baby is always such an exciting time and assembling the first set of clothes a major event in itself. These bright and cheerful daisy motifs are simple to stitch, so can be added to as many pieces as you have time for. The little dress has a slightly larger motif but the designs can be adapted to whatever pieces you have chosen for the layette. I have used just one little daisy on the mittens, as these are so small.

Finished size of stitching:
dress 5.5 × 5 cm (2¼ × 2 in)
pants and hat 4 × 3 cm (1½ × 1¼ in)
mittens 2.3 × 3 cm (⅞ × 1¼ in)

MATERIALS

White waste canvas, 14 count, size 14 × 6 cm
   (5.5 × 2.5 in)

DMC STRANDED COTTON:

1 skein each of

604 baby pink

B5200 snow white

602 dark pink

955 pale aqua

Chenille or embroidery needle
White dress with pants, hat and mittens,
   size 0-3 months

STITCHING INSTRUCTIONS

1 Cut pieces of waste canvas just larger than each of the motifs. Bind or machine zig-zag stitch the edges to avoid snagging the clothes' fabric, following the instructions on page 114. Tack into position on each of the items.

2 Work the design with two strands of cotton for the cross stitches and one strand for the backstitch outlines. I have stitched the group of three flowers on the dress, the pair of flowers on the pants (one side is the reverse of the other) and just the left hand flower from the dress motif on the mittens.

3 Start by cross stitching the stems and leaves, then work the flowers, following the chart on page 21. Complete the motifs by outlining with backstitch.

4 Remove the waste canvas carefully, using tweezers where necessary.

ADAPTATIONS AND VARIATIONS

1 The pink flowers can happily be worked in another colour if preferred, however, for a more lively variation, try stitching each flower in a completely different colour.

2 For more concentrated stitching, these motifs could be repeated around the entire hem of the dress and edges of the hat, pants and mittens. The two different sizes of motifs could be alternated, with one being stitched in a slightly lighter or darker shade than the other.

3 These designs could also be stitched on a cardigan and jacket to complete the co-ordinated set of clothing.

—— 604 baby pink

B5200 snow white

955 pale aqua

604 baby pink

602 dark pink

Rabbit and Bear Tee Shirts

These irresistible rabbit and bear motifs are designed to create a truly individual piece for that special baby's wardrobe. They can be placed together as on this Tee shirt, or for an equally attractive effect, used separately. Attaching them with fusible web and a machine zig-zag stitch means that the motifs can be easily applied to any fabric or piece of clothing, it doesn't have to be traditional evenweave.

Finished size of stitching:
rabbit 5 × 3.5 cm (2 × 1½ in)
bear 4.5 × 5 cm (1¾ × 2 in)

MATERIALS
Blue or white Belfast linen,
    32 count, size 17 × 10 cm
    (7 × 4 in)

DMC STRANDED COTTON:

for navy tee shirt, 1 skein each of

 809 pale blue

727 pale yellow

939 dark navy

for white tee shirt, 1 skein each of

 800 very pale blue

798 blue

820 very dark blue

Tapestry needle, size 26
Fusible web, size 10 × 4.5 cm (4 × 1¾ in)
Plain navy or white Tee shirt, size 3 - 6 months
Matching sewing thread

STITCHING INSTRUCTIONS

1 This project is worked entirely in cross stitch, using two strands of cotton, except for the backstitch to make the rabbit's mouth, which is worked with one strand.

2 Stitch the dark blue outlines and features first, following the chart on page 24 and using the centre lines as a guide for positioning.

3 Fill in the two-colour backgrounds with the appropriate pattern. If the motifs are to be placed overlapping each other, then the bottom left 1 cm (⅜ in) square of the rabbit can be left unstitched.

MAKING UP

1 Trim the pieces of linen to within 1 cm (³⁄₈ in) of the stitching to allow for the turnings. Press these turnings to the wrong side.

2 Cut two pieces of fusible web very slightly smaller than the size of the linen.

3 Iron the fusible web to the wrong side of the stitched pieces. Remove the paper backing and iron in the most appropriate positions on to the tee shirt, using a damp cloth over the stitching.

4 Machine zig-zag around the edges or oversew with small stitches by hand.

ADAPTATIONS AND VARIATIONS

1 Reverse the patterned and unstitched areas, so that the bear and rabbit are filled in and the surrounding areas are left showing the linen fabric. Fill in either with the existing pattern or with just one of the colours as a solid area.

2 Use the motifs separately, perhaps on a whole range of items to make a matching set.

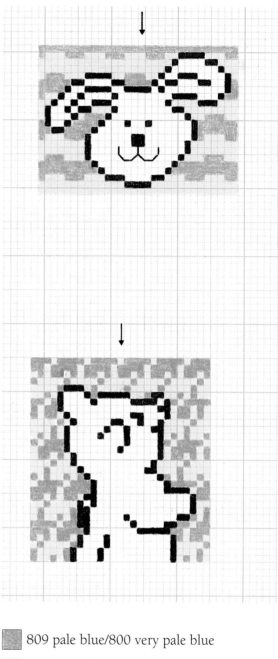

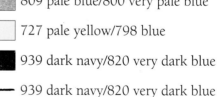

▨	809 pale blue/800 very pale blue
▢	727 pale yellow/798 blue
■	939 dark navy/820 very dark blue
—	939 dark navy/820 very dark blue

Denim Dungarees and Dress

A delightful, versatile motif, stitched in primary colours, perfect for brightening up any item of clothing. This is also an ideal project for using up scraps of threads left over from other projects. The little cars take very little thread and they would look just as much fun if each car was coloured slightly differently.

Finished size of stitching, one car:
3 × 2 cm (1¼ × ¾ in)

MATERIALS

White waste canvas, 14 count, size 5 × 4 cm
(2 × 1½ in) for one car

DMC STRANDED COTTON:

1 skein each of

 666 red

 799 light blue

 911 bright green

Chenille or embroidery needle
Denim dungarees or pinafore dress

STITCHING INSTRUCTIONS

1 Work out the best positions for the cars to be stitched. If this is not immediately obvious, use paper cars pinned to the dungarees and dress to decide. It is better not to choose positions where there are more than two thicknesses of material, or in a very confined space, as this makes stitching very difficult.

2 Using two strands of cotton, work in cross stitch throughout.

3 Attach the waste canvas (see page 114) and, following the chart below, begin stitching from either the front or back end of the car, 1 cm (⅜ in) from the edge of the waste canvas. The three thread colours are used in three different combinations. You can choose which and how many combinations to use depending on the space you have available.

4 Once the stitching is completed, carefully remove the tacking and the waste canvas.

ADAPTATIONS AND VARIATIONS

1 If a larger count of waste canvas is used, e.g. 11 count, then the car would have a finished size of nearly 5 × 2.5 cm (2 × 1 in). This would then be ideal for placing on a central pocket or on the bib section of the dungarees. It could be repeated on a denim jacket and hat to make a matching outfit.

2 This funny little car would be very suitable if stitched in a line along a bib, which could match with a stitched band placed inside a baby's drinking cup. It would also stand out on a towel band with the cars placed close together so that they are touching end to end.

3 Finally, if preferred, this motif could be worked on Aida, then appliquéed onto the chosen item of clothing in the same way as for the rabbit and bear designs on the Tee shirts on page 22.

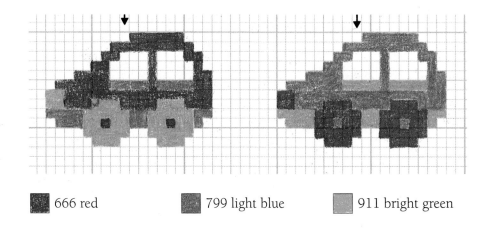

■ 666 red ■ 799 light blue ■ 911 bright green

Nautical Sun Hat

This project provides an essential item for baby's summer holiday: a stylish sun hat. The stitching has been worked on a purchased hat and could easily be extended to other items of clothing to make a coordinated summer wardrobe.

Finished size of stitching, 1 boat:
5.5 cm (2¼ in) square

MATERIALS
White waste canvas, 14 count, size 10 cm (4 in) square for 1 boat

DMC FLOWER THREADS:

1 skein each of

■ 2956 aqua

■ 2820 royal blue

■ 2321 red

■ 2800 baby blue

· blanc white

■ 2823 navy blue

Chenille or embroidery needle
Blue denim sun hat

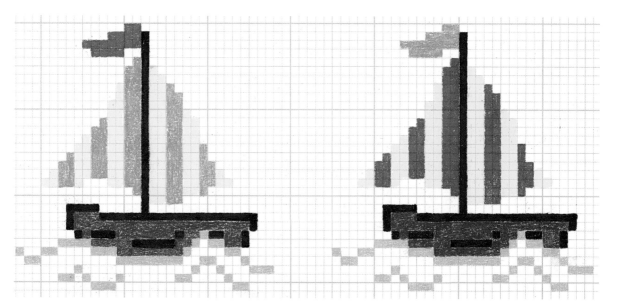

STITCHING INSTRUCTIONS

1 The hat used for this project had eight panels, so I stitched each of the two boats on alternate panels, firstly with blue and white sails, then with red and white.

2 Work in cross stitch using a single strand of flower thread throughout.

3 Cut separate pieces of waste canvas for each motif. Place one of the pieces in the centre of one of the panels and follow the instructions on page 114 to attach and stitch over the canvas.

4 Following the chart on page 28, start stitching the mast and flag of the boat, then the sails, the boat itself, and finally the waves. Carefully remove the waste canvas and tacking.

ADAPTATIONS AND VARIATIONS

This is a versatile motif that could be easily used on baby linen for a nursery or bathroom with a nautical theme. Use it, for example, on bed linen, towels, flannels or a bathrobe.

Simple Socks

Use waste canvas to transform a pair of plain white socks into a bright and colourful item for your favourite baby. The designs can be embroidered onto any size of sock. Each one is quick and easy to stitch, so that you can easily do both and once the baby starts toddling, more than one pair will certainly be needed.

Finished size of stitching:

hearts, depth 1.5 cm (½ in), width varies

spots, depth 2.3 cm (⅞ in), width varies

MATERIALS

White waste canvas, 14 count, size 3.5 cm (1 ¼ in) square for 1- 2 motifs

DMC STRANDED COTTON:

for hearts, 1 skein each of

 818 very pale rose pink

3716 pink

for spots, 1 skein each of

 800 very pale blue

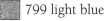 799 light blue

Chenille or embroidery needle
White ankle socks

STITCHING INSTRUCTIONS

1 As the socks are so small, it is easier to stitch through the waste canvas if only small pieces, sufficient for one or two motifs, are attached at a time.

2 Measure the circumference of the sock top in order to determine the spacing of the heart or spot motifs.

3 Attach the waste canvas in the usual way (see page 114), remembering to bind or machine zig-zag the edges to avoid snagging the socks. Do not stretch the ribbing of the socks.

4 Work in cross stitch using two strands of cotton throughout.

5 Cross stitch the chosen design following the chart below.

6 Remove the waste canvas, taking care not to over stretch the sock material.

ADAPTATIONS AND VARIATIONS

A complete outfit featuring these simple motifs could easily be produced by stitching them onto plain coloured Tee shirts, shorts, dresses, pants, etc.

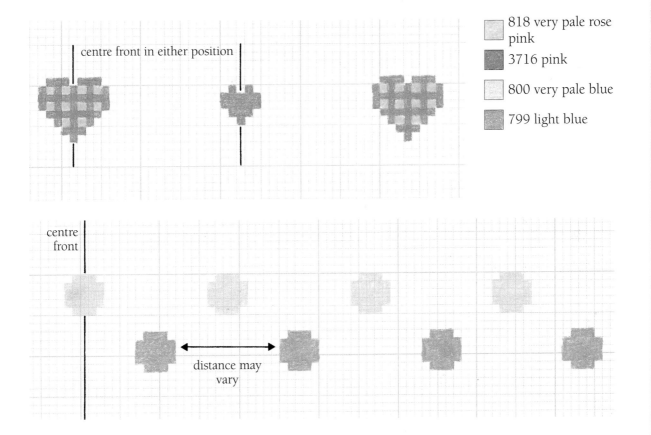

818 very pale rose pink

3716 pink

800 very pale blue

799 light blue

centre front in either position

centre front

distance may vary

Tulip Blouse

Using a fine gauge waste canvas, this simple, yet charming flower motif is easily stitched, giving a personal touch to a purchased blouse. Two shades of pink and lemon threads have been stitched alternately, to create a bright, modern design on a traditionally styled baby blouse. It would also be perfectly suited to make a matching blouse for an older sister.

Finished size of stitching, 1 pair of flowers:
1 × 3 cm (³⁄₈ × 1¹⁄₄ in)

MATERIALS

White waste canvas, 14 count, size 3 × 5 cm
(1¹⁄₄ × 2 in) for one pair of flowers

DMC STRANDED COTTON:

1 skein each of

☐ 745 very pale yellow

◻ 744 light orange

◻ 963 pale sugar pink

◼ 894 clear pink

◻ 564 pale silver green

Chenille or embroidery needle
White blouse

STITCHING INSTRUCTIONS

1 Measure the space between the buttons and check that the two tulips will easily fit. The blouse I used had a 4 cm (1¹⁄₂ in) space. If this is different from your blouse, either stitch only one flower or add a third. Alternatively the gauge of the waste canvas could be changed to make the finished size of the stitching either larger or smaller.

2 Cut a separate piece of waste canvas for each space between the buttons, and a smaller piece for each side of the collar.

3 Following the instructions for using waste canvas on page 114, tack these into position, lining up the centres with the line of buttonholes.

4 All the cross stitching is worked using two strands of cotton. Following the chart opposite, stitch the stalks of the tulips first, making sure that the space between them is in the centre of the space between the buttons.

5 Complete the flowers by working the darker shades first, then the paler ones.

6 Carefully remove the pieces of waste canvas and tacking stitches.

ADAPTATIONS AND VARIATIONS

1 This is an extremely versatile design and could be stitched on any number of different items, in a variety of positions e.g. in a long line along the bottom of a Tee shirt or cardigan or round the yoke of a dress or dungarees.

2 The colours of the flowers can easily be changed to match other items of clothing worn with the blouse. Alternatively, change the colours used here to others already available in your workbox. This is an ideal design for using up leftover threads as the quantities needed are very small.

For the Nursery

Floral Moses Basket Cover

This floral repeat design forms an attractive scalloped shape pattern when stitched several times over, making it ideal for this basket cover. As it is stitched on an Aida band, it can easily be applied to purchased linen for a pram, cot or Moses basket. The delicate, tiny flowers are a perfect design for your newborn baby's first few months.

Finished size of stitching, one repeat:
2 × 3.9 cm (¾ × 1⁹⁄₁₆ in)

MATERIALS

White Aida band, 16 count, 2 cm (¾ in) wide and 1.5 m (1½ yards) long

DMC STRANDED COTTON:

1 skein each of

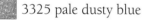 3325 pale dusty blue

826 sea blue

726 pale gold

3078 pale lemon

564 pale silver green

Tapestry needle, size 26
White quilt cover, to fit a Moses basket
White sewing thread

STITCHING INSTRUCTIONS

1 Measure the length of Aida band required to fit the cover, adding on 2 cm (¾ in) extra at both ends.

2 Work in cross stitch throughout, using two strands of cotton.

3 Fold the Aida band in half and mark the centre with tacking stitches. Following the chart below, start stitching a yellow flower in the middle of a scallop at this point.

4 Continue stitching the repeat pattern right and left of the centre position, until the required length is completed.

MAKING UP

1 Pin the Aida band round the curved edge of the quilt cover, gently easing it to fit round the curves.

2 Turn under the raw edges at either end and slip stitch to the cover by hand.

ADAPTATIONS AND VARIATIONS

1 This garland flower design is especially suitable where lengths or bands of stitching are required, for example on pram or cot linen,

round yokes or hems on dresses, jackets, cardigans, and around bonnets or pull-on hats. This stitching could be worked directly onto the item, using waste canvas, or onto the Aida band first as here.

2 The Aida band is available in a variety of different colourways. Not only is there a solid green, blue, pink, lemon and red version, but also there are several white bands with coloured edgings. These could be matched to the colours of stitching worked on the band.

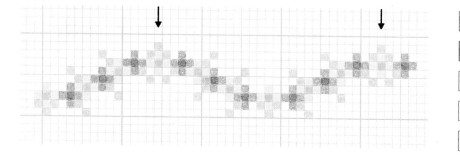

3325 pale dusty blue

826 sea blue

726 pale gold

3078 pale lemon

564 pale silver green

Enchanted Castle Blanket

This fairytale castle in the clouds has transformed the baby blanket into a magical bedtime cover. By using a large mesh size of waste canvas, the design can be quickly completed and, of course, can also be stitched on the baby's cot sheet to create a matching set.

Finished size of stitching:
approximately 16 × 25 cm (6 ¼ in × 10 in)

MATERIALS
White waste canvas, 9 count, size 26 × 35 cm (10 × 14 in)

DMC STRANDED COTTON:

1 skein each of

794 pale royal blue

796 dark blue

964 light aqua

959 aqua

958 medium aqua

943 dark aqua

210 light mauve

209 pale mauve

605 very pale pink

745 very pale yellow

Chenille or embroidery needle
White or cream cot blanket

STITCHING INSTRUCTIONS

1 As described on page 114, it is a good idea to enclose the edges of the waste canvas, to prevent it from damaging the blanket as you are stitching.

2 Tack the waste canvas to the blanket, in the bottom right hand corner.

3 All the cross stitching uses three strands of cotton, while the short line of backstitching is worked in one strand.

4 Start in the centre of the chart on page 44 and complete the castle before beginning the clouds. Finish the design by back stitching the outlines on the castle.

5 Remove the waste canvas, following the instructions on page 114 and taking special care not to damage the surface of the blanket. As the waste canvas used here has thicker threads than the ones used in other projects, tweezers will be needed throughout.

ADAPTATIONS AND VARIATIONS

1 Perlé cotton would be a suitable alternative thread to use here. It is slightly thicker and has an attractive sheen when stitched. The outlining would have to be worked in the finer no. 8, instead of the usual no. 5 which would be used for the main motif.

2 If this design is being used for a smaller blanket for a pram, a finer waste canvas, e.g.14 count, may be preferable. This would reduce the overall size of the stitching to approximately 10×16 cm ($4 \times 6\frac{1}{2}$ in).

3 The size of this design makes it very suitable for a decorative cushion on a nursery chair. Using the same size of waste canvas, it could be stitched on to any plain fabric, perhaps one already used in the nursery. Alternatively, work the design directly onto Aida or other evenweave fabric. There is an 8 count Aida, which would make the overall size slightly larger, or an 11 count, which would work out slightly smaller. Several 18 count evenweaves are available on which the stitches could be worked over two threads.

794 pale royal blue	958 medium aqua	605 very pale pink
796 dark blue	943 dark aqua	745 very pale yellow
964 light aqua	210 light mauve	— 958 medium aqua
959 aqua	209 pale mauve	

Bunny Rabbit Hand Towel

Transform a plain white towel with this line of very smartly dressed rabbits. The design is worked on a cotton Aida band, then appliquéed onto the towel. The length of the band can be adapted to fit any size of towel and the number of rabbits can then be adjusted to fit the space available.

Finished size of stitching, 1 rabbit:
3 × 6.5 cm (1¼ × 2½ in)

MATERIALS

White Aida band, 8.5 cm (3⅜ in) wide, 45 cm (18 in) long

DMC STRANDED COTTON:

1 skein each of

754 very pale salmon pink

813 light sea blue

3756 very pale blue

722 dull orange

948 creamy pink

826 sea blue

Tapestry needle, size 24
White towel, width 41 cm (16 in)
White sewing thread

STITCHING INSTRUCTIONS

1 Fold the Aida band in half, short sides together, to find the centre. Mark this with a line of tacking stitches.

2 Work the cross stitching using two strands of cotton and the backstitching with one strand. The only exception is the rabbit's mouth, which is stitched with two strands.

3 Following the chart on page 46, start by stitching the centre rabbit.

4 When the centre rabbit is completed, work out how many rabbits on either side you will have room for, if your band is not the same length as the one shown. You will need 15 holes for each rabbit and an even number between them. Measure the space between the arms and keep this constant. The girl teddy bear has a slightly wider skirt but this can extend into the space between the bears.

5 Mark the position of each rabbit with tacking stitches, then work outwards from the centre.

MAKING UP

1 Trim the ends of the Aida band to 2 cm (¾ in) longer than the towel. Remove all tacking threads apart from the line marking the centre. Fold the towel in half, long sides together and mark the centre with pins.

2 Pin and tack the stitched band to one short edge of the towel, lining up the centre of the towel with the centre of the band. Turn in a hem at both ends of the band level with the towel and pin or tack.

3 Either machine or hand stitch all round the outer edges of the band, until it is firmly attached. Remove the tacking thread.

ADAPTATIONS AND VARIATIONS

1 Stitch these mischievous looking rabbits separately on other towelling products to make a co-ordinated set, for example on a flannel, a towel mitt and the pocket of baby's dressing gown.

2 Stitched separately, these rabbits would look perfect on a greetings card either to celebrate a new birth or for a birthday.

— 722 dull orange

— 826 sea blue

▨ 754 very pale salmon pink

▨ 813 light sea blue

□ 3756 very pale blue

▨ 722 dull orange

□ 948 creamy pink

46

Pig and Ducks Cushion

A lively design depicting favourite animals, sure to delight any baby or toddler. The central motif is worked on a square of Aida, which is then framed with a duck border stitched on a length of Aida band with a matching yellow edging. The bright colour combination will make this cushion a versatile item for many a nursery.

Finished size of stitching:
23 cm (9 in) square

Finished size of cushion:
35.5 cm (14 in) square

MATERIALS
White Aida, 14 count, size 22.5 cm (5 in)
  square

White Aida band with yellow trim, 5 cm (2 in)
  wide, 1 m (40 in) long

DMC STRANDED COTTON:

1 skein each of

☐ 819 very pale pink

▨ 776 rose pink

2 skeins of

☐ 745 very pale yellow

Tapestry needle, size 24
White lining fabric, 1 piece, 23 cm (9 in) square
Co-ordinating cushion fabric, 2 pieces, 39 cm
  (15½ in) square
Matching sewing thread
Cushion pad, 35 cm (14 in) square

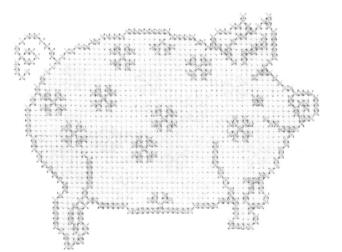

48

STITCHING INSTRUCTIONS

1 The pig and the ducks are worked in cross stitch, using two strands of cotton throughout.

2 Using the square of white Aida and following the chart on page 51, start by stitching the outline of the pig, then stitch the yellow and pink flowers. Finally fill in the background.

3 Using the white Aida band, stitch the duck border. Start with duck number 1, approximately 8 cm (3¼ in) from the end of the Aida band. Stitch ducks 1, 2 and 3, then measure 22 cm (8¾ in) from the centre of duck 2 to position the centre of duck 5. Now stitch ducks 4, 5 and 6. Again measure 22 cm (8¾ in), this time from the centre of duck 5 to position the centre of duck 8. Continue as before, until all the ducks are stitched.

MAKING UP

1 Place the stitched duck band on the embroidered square, so that the pig design is central with a 1 cm (½ in) unstitched area at

either side. Mark the corners, which will be mitred, with pins. The band and square should measure approximately 23 cm (9 in) square. Remove the band, fold the mitres to the wrong side, pin the stitching line and machine stitch in place. Cut away the excess fabric of the seam, leaving 1 cm (⅜ in) on either seam.

2 Replace the band in position on the square of Aida and machine stitch on the inside edge of the band.

3 Place this panel centrally on top of the square of white lining fabric, right sides up. This will ensure that the colour and pattern of the cushion fabric will not show through the stitched Aida. Place these two pieces centrally on top of one piece of the cushion fabric and pin in place.

4 Secure these three layers together by machine stitching along the outside edge of the Aida band.

5 Place these pieces centrally over the second piece of cushion fabric, right sides together. Machine stitch together 1.5 cm (⅝ in) from the edge and leaving a 25 cm (10 in) gap along the bottom edge.

6 Turn right side out and make sure the corners are fully pulled through. Insert the cushion pad and slip stitch the gap closed.

ADAPTATIONS AND VARIATIONS

1 The band could be stitched with evenly spaced ducks and used to decorate a towel, bib, sheet or curtain edge and tie-back.

2 Alternatively, a single duck motif would be ideal for decorating any item of clothing, using waste canvas, e.g. hat, socks, shirt, jacket, dungarees, dress, nightwear.

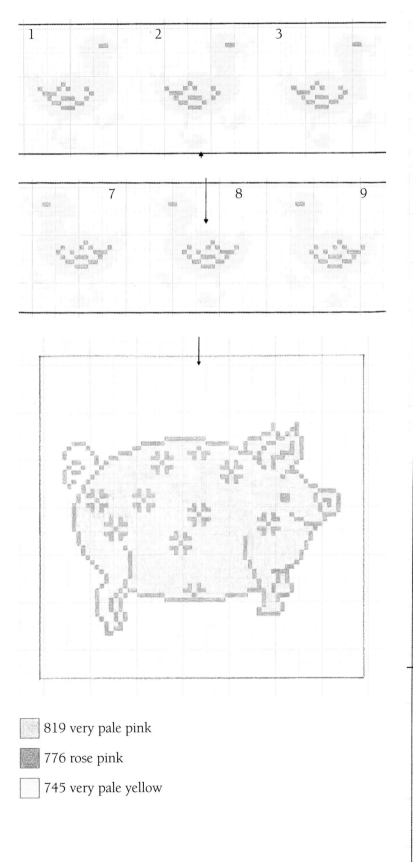
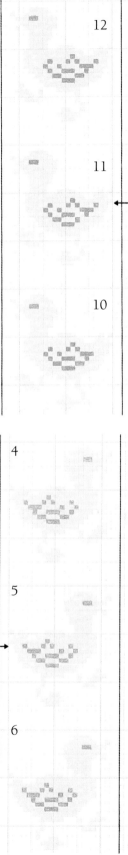

819 very pale pink

776 rose pink

745 very pale yellow

Smiley Sheep Cot Linen

Add these attractive motifs to transform plain cot linen for that very special baby. Pale green is a soothing colour and counting sheep is meant to be conducive to sleep. The designs are worked on Aida then appliquéed to the linen using fusible web and machine stitching, so any number of motifs can easily be attached. If you are working by hand, the motifs can be finished with an edging of buttonhole stitch.

Finished size of stitching:
sheet approximately 10 × 7.5 cm (4 × 3 in)
pillow case approximately 5.5 × 4 cm
   (2¼ × 1½ in)

MATERIALS

Green fine Aida, 18 count, size 25 × 13 cm
   (10 × 5 in) for the pillowcase
Green fine Aida, 18 count, size 15 × 18 cm
   (6 × 7 in) for the sheet

DMC STRANDED COTTON:

1 skein each of

☐ white

■ 792 royal blue

▨ 913 pale bright green

Tapestry needle, size 26
Iron-on fusible web, size 25 × 13 cm (10 × 5 in)
Cot sheet and pillowcase
Green sewing thread

STITCHING INSTRUCTIONS

1 All the cross stitching in blue is worked with one strand of cotton and all the white cross stitching with two strands of cotton. The backstitching used for the mouths is worked with one strand of the blue cotton.

2 For the sheet motif, follow the chart on page 54. First cross stitch the blue outlines of the sheep, then the swirls and the feet.

3 Fill in the sheep with the white cross stitches and finish by stitching the mouth outlines in back stitch. Work the grass in cross stitch to complete.

4 For the pillowcase motif, work in exactly the same way but just stitch the smaller sheep (I have worked it in reverse) and stitch tufts of grass on either side of the hooves.

MAKING UP

1 Trace the outline shape of the motifs on page 122 onto the fusible web, then iron on to the back of the stitched Aida, making sure the stitching is central.

2 Now cut carefully through all layers following the drawn outlines.

3 Peel away the paper backing and iron the motifs onto the sheet and pillowcase, using a damp cloth on top of the stitching.

4 Using a close zig-zag stitch, machine around the motifs, covering the raw edges. Alternatively, work in blanket stitch by hand.

ADAPTATIONS AND VARIATIONS

1 Machine embroidery thread made from rayon has an attractive sheen and can be used for the machine edging, as an alternative to the usual cotton.

2 The cot sheet and pillowcase can easily be made up from cotton sheeting, instead of being bought. This gives the opportunity to add some additional decorative stitching, such as the green scalloped line seen on the pillowcase.

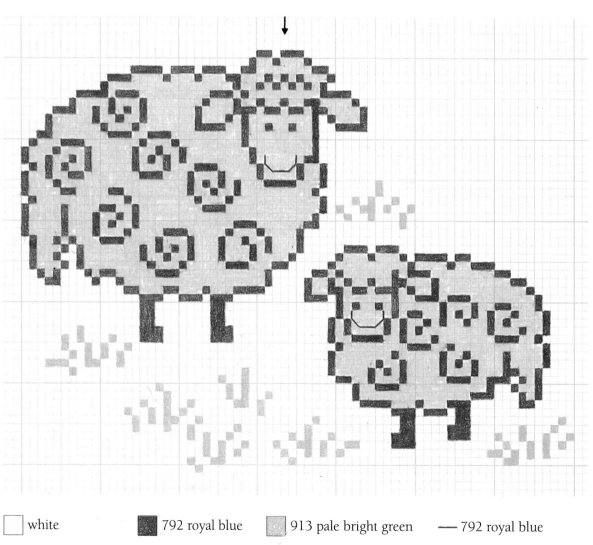

| | white | | 792 royal blue | | 913 pale bright green | —— 792 royal blue |

Teddy Bear Cot Quilt

Add that special finishing touch to the nursery with this beautiful cot quilt, made up of a central stitched panel, surrounded by fabric borders. These adorable bears, a favourite toy of so many children are stitched in a variety of colourful checks. Butterflies, bees and flowers are scattered around the bears, with more butterflies stitched through waste canvas on to the borders. This is a fairly complex project but the results will be all the more treasured.

Finished size of stitched centre panel:
35.5 × 57 cm (14 × 22½ in)

Finished size of quilt:
58 × 80 cm (23 × 31½ in)

MATERIALS
Cream Cashel Linen 28 count, size 48 × 69 cm
   (19 × 27 in)
White waste canvas, 28 count, size 12 cm
   (4.5 in) square

DMC STRANDED COTTON:

2 skeins each of

⬛ 799 light blue

⬜ 959 aqua

3 skeins each of

⬜ 743 orange yellow

⬛ 962 deep pink

4 skeins each of

⬛ 3750 dark air force blue

Tapestry needle, size 24
Chenille or embroidery needle
Cream fabric for borders and backing, size
    87 × 111 cm (34¼ × 43¾ in)
4 oz polyester wadding, size 58 × 82 cm
    (23 × 32¼ in)
Cream sewing thread

STITCHING INSTRUCTIONS

1 Work all the cross stitching using two strands of cotton and all the backstitching with one strand.

2 In the techniques section, I recommend using a suitably sized frame for most of the projects. However, when stitching the centre panel of this quilt, the larger the frame, the better. In fact, a floor frame is ideal: very little of the stitching would need to be rolled around the frame bars, so that you will be able to see almost all of the design as you stitch. This will help you to place the different colourways.

3 On the linen, mark an unstitched border of 5 cm (2 in) on each side with lines of tacking stitches. Following the chart on page 58, start stitching the backstitched outline of one square in the top left hand corner, taking care to position this first square correctly.

4 Next backstitch the flowers in each of the corners of the square, then the butterfly and bee in backstitch and cross stitch.

5 Finally, stitch the bear, working all the outlines before filling in with the checks.

6 Continue stitching each square, taking care to use the correct colours for the check patterns, butterflies, bees and flowers.

7 For the borders, cut four pieces of border fabric the length of each side plus 15 cm (6 in). Tack on a 6 cm (2½ in) square piece of waste canvas (see page 114) for each butterfly and stitch following the single butterfly chart on page 58. On the long sides, there is one blue and yellow butterfly in the centre and one at each end of the top and bottom horizontal lines of the quilt, facing towards the quilt. On the short sides, there is one aqua and pink butterfly just to the left and another just to the right of the vertical lines, both facing to the centre of the border.

8 Once all the stitching is completed, carefully remove the pieces of waste canvas and tacking.

MAKING UP

1 Remove the linen from the frame and trim the unstitched fabric to within 2.5 cm (1 in) of the design. Machine zig-zag or use pinking shears on the edges to prevent excess fraying of the linen while you are making up the quilt.

2 Pin and stitch the borders to the quilt, taking a 1.5 cm (⅝ in) seam allowance and leaving the mitres free. Pin and stitch the mitres. Trim the seams.

3 Cut a piece of the backing fabric measuring 61 × 85 cm (24 × 33½ in).

4 Lay the stitched piece centrally on top of the wadding and pin.

5 Lay the backing fabric on top of the stitched panel, right sides together and pin. Stitch round all four sides, taking a 1.5 cm (⅝ in) seam allowance and leaving a 25 cm (10 in) gap in one of the sides. Trim the seams.

6 Turn the quilt right side out, making sure the corners are well pulled through and slip stitch the gap closed.

7 Using safety pins or tacking stitches, secure the three layers in a grid of horizontal, vertical and diagonal lines, so that it will not pucker as you machine quilt.

8 Machine stitch round all four sides of the inner border.

ADAPTATIONS AND VARIATIONS

1 One square of this design is ideal for stitching on one of the range of blankets or shawls with evenweave panels designed for cross stitch. A different colourway could be stitched in each of the panels or the bear motif could be alternated with the border butterfly.

2 There is a wide variety of wooden boxes available, designed specifically to have a piece of stitching inserted in the lid. Use this teddy motif to make a perfect box to hold baby's treasures.

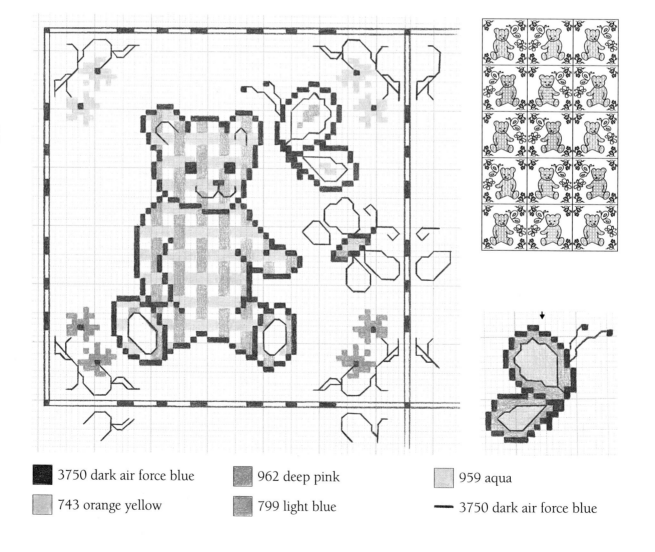

	3750 dark air force blue		962 deep pink		959 aqua
	743 orange yellow		799 light blue	—	3750 dark air force blue

Bathtime Hooded Towel

This hooded towel, decorated with five easily recognisable motifs, is the ideal way of keeping baby warm, cosy and dry after bathtime.

Finished size of stitching:
26 × 7 cm (10¼ × 2¾ in)

MATERIALS
Hooded towel with 14 count Aida panel on the hood, size 68 × 76 cm (27 × 30 in)

DMC STRANDED COTTON:

1 skein each of

■	827 pale sea blue
■	334 dusty blue
□	775 very pale dusty blue
■	964 light aqua
■	958 medium aqua
■	742 pale orange
□	3078 pale lemon
□	743 orange yellow
■	322 dark dusty blue
□	white

Tapestry needle, size 24
Bias binding in a matching colour
Matching sewing thread

STITCHING INSTRUCTIONS

1 Mark the centre of the Aida triangle with a tacking thread. Use this and the centre mark on the chart to position the outline of the middle block.

2 All cross and back stitching is worked using two strands of cotton.

3 Following the chart below, stitch the central motif, then stitch the background. Once this is completed, stitch the outlines of the other four blocks in the same way (motif first, then background).

4 To complete the design, work the waves beneath the motifs in cross stitch.

ADAPTATIONS AND VARIATIONS

1 An alternative to buying one of these hooded towels is to make one with towelling and Aida. This gives the opportunity to use a coloured towel and attach a patterned binding round the edges. A checked binding would look particularly effective.

2 The motifs could be used separately or in groups of two and three on other bathtime items. DMC produce a range of Aida shapes with finished edges, ready to appliqué onto any item of your choice. The motifs used on this hooded towel would be ideal for these.

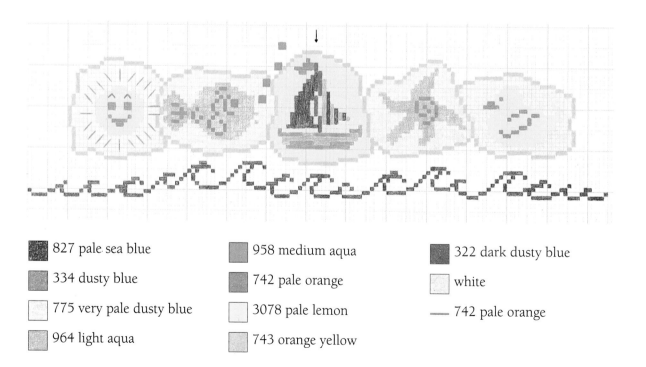

■ 827 pale sea blue	■ 958 medium aqua	■ 322 dark dusty blue
■ 334 dusty blue	■ 742 pale orange	□ white
□ 775 very pale dusty blue	□ 3078 pale lemon	— 742 pale orange
■ 964 light aqua	■ 743 orange yellow	

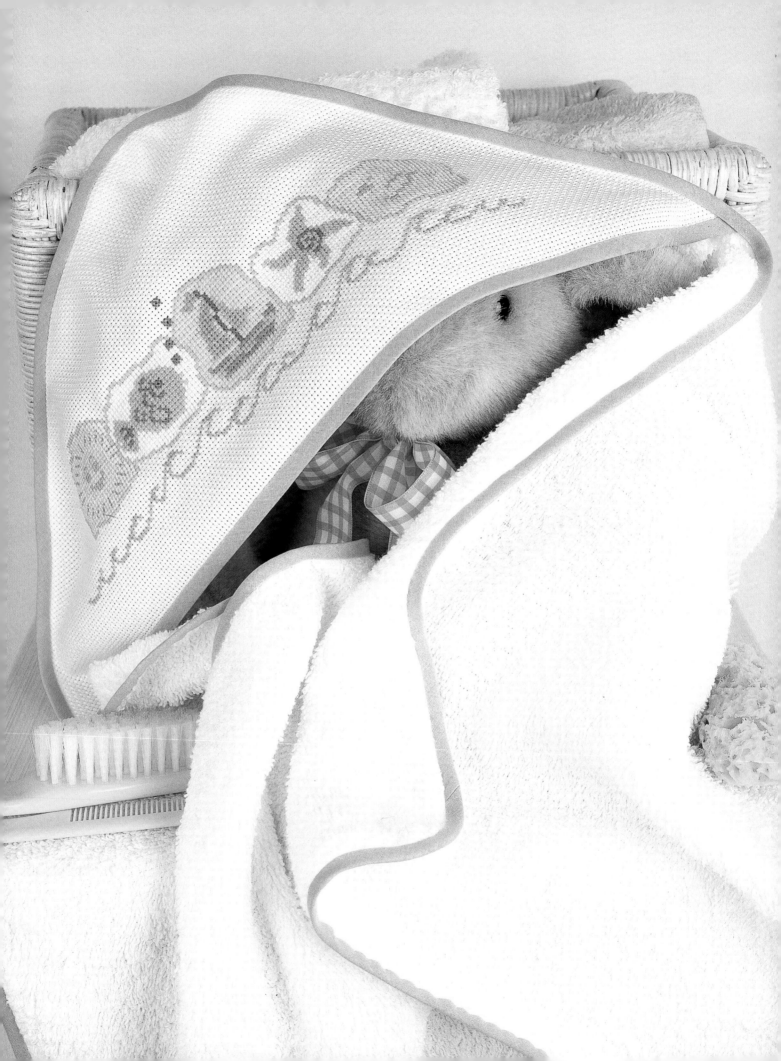

Sunflower Baby Tidy

These cheerful flowers will brighten up any nursery. Use as a tidy for baby's small toys and tie to the cot, so that they can be easily reached. Alternatively, store useful items, such as brushes, combs, cotton wool balls and safety pins, and attach to the nursery wall, a cupboard door or a chair. To create a different length of band, simply stitch more or fewer panels.

Finished size of stitching, 1 motif:
approximatley 6 × 8.5 cm (2½ × 3½ in)

Finished size of tidy:
38 × 25 cm (15 × 10 in)

MATERIALS
White linen band, 13 count, 12 cm (4¾ in) wide, 68 cm (27 in) long

DMC STRANDED COTTON:

1 skein each of

- 3825 salmon pink
- 744 light orange
- 722 dull orange
- 993 turquoise
- 964 light aqua
- 3823 ivory
- 721 dark orange

Tapestry needle, size 24
Yellow and white gingham
    fabric, size 38×25 cm
    (14×10 in)
White cotton backing
    fabric, size 38×25 cm
    (14×10 in)
Plain yellow fabric/bias
    binding, length 3 m
    (3 yards)
Matching sewing thread

STITCHING INSTRUCTIONS

1 Mark the central positions of the three flowers on the linen band, with a tacking thread. The distance between these should be 20 cm (8 in).

2 Following the chart below, complete each flower, stalk and leaves, using two strands of cotton for the cross stitch and one strand for the outlining in back stitch.

3 Stitch the flower pots, starting with the rims behind the flowers, then completing the patterns, before stitching the backgrounds.

MAKING UP

1 Fold and iron the stitched band, making inverted pleats in between the motifs and a single pleat at either end. The width of each embroidered panel is 12 cm (4⅜ in). Trim away the excess linen at the ends, leaving a seam allowance of 1 cm (⅜ in).

2 Place the piece of gingham on top of the piece of white backing fabric, right sides up, then position the pleated band on the gingham, right sides up, lining up the bottom edges. Tack the pieces together round the edges.

3 To make the ties, cut two lengths of bias binding, 71 cm (28 in) long, fold in half lengthways and slip stitch along the sides.

4 Stitch bias binding around the edges of the tidy. Fold the ties in half and stitch them to the top of the tidy on the wrong side. Remove all tacking.

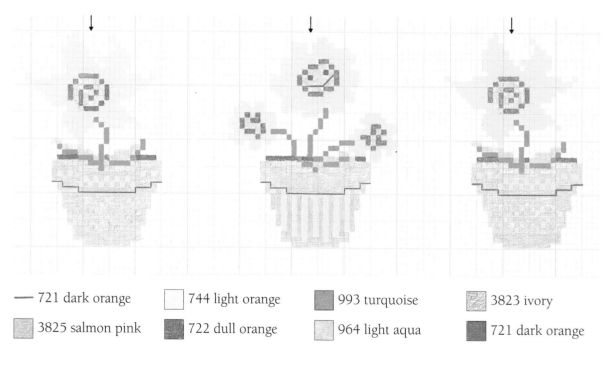

— 721 dark orange	☐ 744 light orange	▨ 993 turquoise	▨ 3823 ivory
▨ 3825 salmon pink	▨ 722 dull orange	☐ 964 light aqua	▨ 721 dark orange

ADAPTATIONS AND VARIATIONS

1 A delightful matching cushion to this tidy could be easily made using the Aida band across the centre and the yellow checked fabric either side.

2 For a completely different idea, these sunny flowers without the flower pots would look lovely on a birthday cake band. Use a 5 cm (2 in) Aida band, either in white or one of the available colours and stitch the two different flower designs alternately. This birthday band could then be washed and re-used for several birthdays to come.

Dinosaur Toy Bag

Any young toddler will delight in having this lovable dinosaur family stitched on a bag designed to hold his or her favourite toys. And if they already have a collection of dinosaur models, the bag will be the perfect gift. The colouring of each dinosaur is slightly different and all five shades of green and yellow have been randomly mixed to create the border, which is worked in double-sized stitches.

Finished size of stitching:
36×9 cm (14×3½ in)

Finished size of tidy:
23 cm (9 in) in diameter, 40 cm (15½ in) high

MATERIALS

White Aida, 14 count, size 44×19 cm (17½×7½ in)

DMC STRANDED COTTON:

1 skein each of

☐ 445 lemon

▨ 726 pale gold

☐ 703 pale green

☐ 772 pale moss green

▨ 906 medium green

■ 904 dark green

Tapestry needle, size 24
Green checked fabric, 2 pieces, each size
    39×41.5 cm (15×16 in)
Yellow cotton fabric, 1 circle, 26 cm (10¼ in) in diameter
Yellow bias binding, length 1.5 m (1½ yards)
Matching sewing thread
Yellow twisted cord, 1 m (1 yard)

STITCHING INSTRUCTIONS

1 All the cross stitching uses two strands of cotton and the small amount of back stitched detail is worked with one strand.

2 Mark the centre of the Aida with a tacking thread and start cross stitching one of the larger dinosaurs, following the chart on page 68.

3 Next stitch the other large dinosaur, followed by the two smaller ones at either end of the design.

4 Complete the dinosaurs by working the back stitching detail on the legs, mouths and twigs.

5 The final step is to cross stitch the borders. These are worked using a random selection of all the thread colours. Each stitch extends over two Aida threads, instead of the usual one thread, and uses two strands of cotton.

MAKING UP

1 Fold over the top and bottom edges of the Aida, leaving a 1 cm (⅜ in) border of unstitched area showing on the right side.

2 Trim the folded edges and the two sides to 1.5 cm (⅜ in). Tack the hems.

3 Place the Aida band on the right side of one of the pieces of checked fabric, 7 cm (2¾ in) up from the bottom short edge. Pin and machine stitch in position.

4 Place this piece of checked fabric on top of the second piece, right sides together. Pin

and machine stitch together down the long sides, taking a 1.5 cm (⅝ in) seam. Trim the seams and machine zig zag stitch to neaten.

5 Pin the yellow circle to the bottom of the tube, right sides together, then machine stitch together, taking a 1.5 cm (⅝ in) seam. Trim and neaten the raw edges as before.

6 Cut the bias binding in half and use one piece to enclose the raw edges at the top of the bag.

7 Pin and machine stitch the other half of the binding to the inside of the bag approximately 5 cm (2 in) from the top.

8 Unpick the seam on one side of the bag between the lines of machine stitching used to attach the bias binding. Insert the cord through this gap, then knot the ends.

ADAPTATIONS AND VARIATIONS

The colours of the threads have been selected to match the green checked fabric. These, however, could be changed to more traditional baby pastel colours if preferred, or to any combination of colours to coordinate with the chosen fabric.

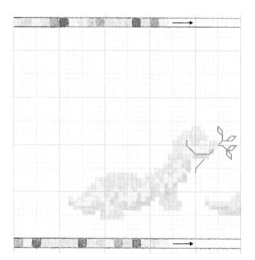

☐	445 lemon
▨	726 pale gold
☐	703 pale green
☐	772 pale moss green
■	906 medium green
▬	904 dark green
▭	703 pale green

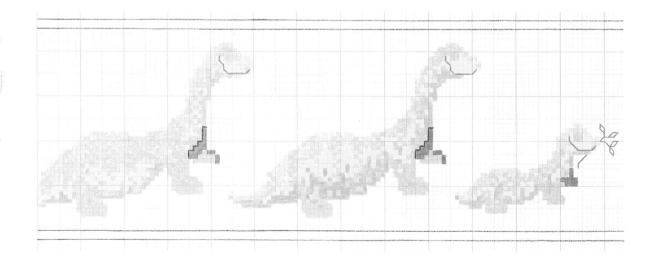

Daisy Curtain Trim and Buttercup Tieback

Preparing and decorating a room for a new baby can be great fun, especially when colours and furnishings are co-ordinated with cross stitch embroidery. Create an eye-catching and truly original window treatment by stitching these attractive buttercups and daisies. The designs have been based on the pattern of the curtain fabric but would look just as effective with a plain colour for the curtain. Dimensions are given for the curtain in the photograph but as the daisy curtain trim is a repeat pattern, the length of the stitching can be varied to fit any size of window. It can be attached to a ready-made curtain or to one you are making yourself. The tieback is of a suitable size for a single width curtain.

Finished size of stitching, 1 daisy motif for curtain:
6 × 8.5 cm (2½ × 3¼ in)

Finished size of stitching, tieback:
8 × 47 cm (3 × 18½ in)

Finished size of curtain:
125 × 115 cm (49¼ × 45¼ in)

Finished size of tieback:
approximately 46 × 9.5 cm (18 × 3¾ in)

MATERIALS

For one curtain trim

Cream linen, 32 count, 28 cm (11 in) wide and the length of the actual curtain plus 15 cm (6 in) hem allowance

DMC STRANDED COTTON:

1 skein of

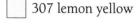 992 sea green

2 skeins each of

☐ 307 lemon yellow

☐ 703 pale green

☐ 907 lime green

☐ 912 medium bright green

☐ 958 medium aqua

☐ 964 light aqua

☐ 3801 new red

☐ 3819 yellow gold

3 skeins each of

☐ 3705 coral pink

☐ 3706 pale coral pink

☐ 3814 dull jewel green

Tapestry needle, size 26
Anna French Buttercups and Daisies, colour 23
  or chosen fabric, 150 cm (60 in) wide and
  1.5 m (1¾ yards) long
Cream curtain lining, 150 cm (60 in) wide and
  1.5 m (1¾ yards) long
Pencil pleat curtain heading tape, 1.5 m
  (1¾ yards)
Curtain interlining (optional), 150 cm (60 in)
  wide and 1.5 m (1¾ yards) long
Matching sewing thread

For one tieback

Cream linen, 32 count, size 61 × 36 cm
  (24 × 14 in) for the tieback

DMC STRANDED COTTON:

1 skein each of

☐ 913 pale bright green

☐ 3812 jewel green

☐ 958 medium aqua

☐ 704 lime green

☐ 742 pale orange

☐ 746 cream

☐ 964 light aqua

☐ 743 orange yellow

☐ 744 light orange

☐ 3078 pale lemon

☐ 993 turquoise

☐ 741 medium orange

☐ 943 dark aqua

Tapestry needle, size 26
Cream curtain lining, size 51 × 18 cm (20 × 7 in)
Pelmet buckram, size 47 × 15 cm (18½ × 6 in)
Curtain interlining, size 47 × 15 cm (18½ × 6 in)
Piping cord, 1.3 m (1½ yards) long, optional
Matching sewing thread
2 brass rings, diameter 2 cm (¾ in)

STITCHING INSTRUCTIONS

Curtain Trim

1 Measure the exact length of trim required and work out the number of whole daisies which will fit, remembering to allow for the unstitched areas at top and bottom which will be seamed.

2 Work in cross stitch throughout using two strands of cotton.

3 Start stitching the first daisy in the correct position at the bottom of the linen, following the chart on page 73.

4 Stitch all the daisies and leaves, ensuring that the outer edges of the design are in line. Note that for the leaves, every alternate motif is reversed.

Tieback

1 Run a line of tacking stitches through the vertical centre of the piece of linen. Start stitching the left side of the tieback, following the chart on page 73 and using two strands of cotton throughout.

2 Once the left side is completed, reverse the chart and stitch the right side.

MAKING UP

Curtain Trim

1 Make up the lined curtain, adding interlining if liked, and attaching a pencil pleat heading tape.

2 Trim the width of the stitched daisies panel to 11.5 cm (4½ in) wide.

3 Fold under the 1.5 cm (⅝ in) seam allowance on both sides and at the top and bottom of this panel, then press flat. Place on top of the made-up curtain and pin into position.

4 Attach to the curtain by machine stitching close to the edges on both sides, then slip stitch by hand across the bottom and top.

Tieback

1 Using the template on page 122, cut the stitched linen to shape, adding a 1.5 cm (⅝ in) seam allowance all the way around. Cut a piece of curtain lining to the same size.

2 Cut the exact size of the template in the buckram and curtain interlining. Dampen the buckram.

3 Place the interlining on top of the buckram, then place the stitched linen on top of the interlining, right sides up.

4 Snip the linen to lie flat around the curves, then secure to the buckram by pressing with an iron.

5 Place the lining onto the back of the tieback, fold in the snipped seam allowance and slip stitch to the linen. Piping cord covered with the curtain fabric could be added if liked.

6 Sew on two brass rings, approximately 1 cm (½ in) from the ends.

ADAPTATIONS AND VARIATIONS

1 Either the daisies or the buttercups could be stitched on to a band of linen or Aida and used with the curtain fabric to make a decorative square cushion. A bolster-shaped cushion would also look attractive with a stitched band, perhaps with one at either end.

2 A stitched picture bow would add to the co-ordinated look of the nursery. Use either a linen or Aida band and attach onto a length of the curtain fabric. Alternatively, stitch the motifs on a piece of linen or Aida, then neaten the edges with a piping made from the curtain fabric.

3 A row of the buttercups could be stitched onto linen, then made up into coat hangers.

	992 sea green
	307 lemon yellow
	703 pale green
	907 lime green
	912 medium bright green
	958 medium aqua
	964 light aqua
	3801 new red
	3819 yellow gold
	3705 coral pink
	3706 pale coral pink
	3814 dull jewel green

Tieback

	913 pale bright green
	3812 jewel green
	958 medium aqua
	704 lime green
	742 pale orange
	746 cream
	964 light aqua
	743 orange yellow
	744 light orange
	3078 pale lemon
	993 turquoise
	741 medium orange
	943 dark aqua

Toys and Gifts

Pram Teddies

Stitch this line of "boys and girls" in shades of blue and pink to make a delightful pram toy. Change the number of teddies to fit any size of cradle, cot or push-chair. The backs of these bears have been finished with a co-ordinating coloured felt with "pinked" edges. However, to make the toy reversible, if you have a twin-ended pram, for example, repeat the stitching as for the front.

Finished size of stitching, 1 teddy:
5.5 × 9 cm (2 × 3½ in)

Finished size of teddy:
6.5 × 10 cm (2½ × 4 in)

MATERIALS
White Belfast linen, 32 count, size 11.5 × 15 cm
(4½ × 6 in) for 1 teddy

DMC STRANDED COTTON:

1 skein each of

	335 medium rose pink
	3716 pink
	3325 pale dusty blue
	809 pale blue
	798 blue

Tapestry needle, size 26
Pieces of blue felt, size 8 × 12 cm (3 × 5 in) for
    1 teddy
White sewing thread
Polyester wadding for stuffing
String elastic, 1 m (39 in)
Large-eyed needle

STITCHING INSTRUCTIONS

1 Following the chart on page 80 and using one strand of thread throughout, cross stitch the bear outline first.

2 Fill in the face markings, then the straps, buttons and spots, all in cross stitch.

3 Complete the bear by cross stitching the background and bow. Repeat for the remaining bears.

MAKING UP

1 Using the template provided on page 122, draw round each bear, having first positioned the stitching centrally. Cut out carefully on the marked lines.

2 Cut a piece of felt for each bear slightly larger than the stitched linen, the edges will be cut to the exact size with the pinking shears at a later stage.

3 Turn under approximately 0.5 - 0.75 cm (¼ - ⅜ in) of linen on each bear to the wrong side and secure in place by pressing with a hot iron.

4 Pin into position on the felt and machine stitch close to the folded edge, leaving a small opening at the bottom, approximately 2 cm (1 in) long.

5 Place the stuffing in the bear and backstitch by hand across the opening.

6 Trim the excess felt with pinking shears close to the machine stitching.

7 Thread the elastic through the middle of each bear with a large-eyed needle, knotting in between each bear, if liked.

8 Fold over the elastic at both ends and bind with several stitches to make loops and use these to attach the string of teddies to the pram, Moses basket or cot.

Adaptations and Variations

1 This project is ideal for using up small pieces of linen, which of course could be different colours. Equally, the pieces of backing felt do not have to be identical.

2 Pieces of patterned fabric could be used instead of the felt and could be attached to the stitched linen right sides together, then turned to the right side before stuffing. Alternatively, the linen and patterned fabric could be attached wrong sides together, then the edges finished with decorative binding or satin ribbon.

3 These light padded bears could also be used for a mobile. As described above, they could also be finished with felt, fabric or stitched backs.

4 An individual bear could be stitched and made up, with a loop of ribbon inserted at the top, so that it could be suspended over the pram or cot.

■	335 medium rose pink
■	3716 pink
□	3325 pale dusty blue
■	809 pale blue
■	798 blue

Cherub Greetings Card

Stitch this lovely card as a special way of welcoming the new baby, or for the memorable Christening Day. The design is given in a choice of two colourways, appropriate for a little boy or girl.

Finished size of stitching:
6.5 cm (2½ in) square

MATERIALS

White Belfast Linen, 32 count, size 12 cm (4½ in) square, for one card

DMC STRANDED COTTON:

for either colourway, 1 skein each of

☐ 745 very pale yellow

☐ 758 very pale maroon

☐ 353 pale salmon pink

☐ 3770 pale creamy pink

☐ 743 orange yellow

☐ white

☐ 762 pale silver

☐ 564 pale silver green

☐ 415 silver

plus, for pink colourway, 1 skein each of

☐ 776 rose pink

☐ 819 very pale pink

plus, for blue colourway, 1 skein each of

☐ 3325 pale dusty blue

☐ 775 very pale dusty blue

Tapestry needle, size 26
Grey/stone card, square aperture, minimum size 6.8 cm (2⅝ in)
Pink card, round aperture, minimum size 8 cm (3⅛ in)
Double-sided sticky tape
2 oz polyester wadding, size 8 cm (3⅛ in), for one card

STITCHING INSTRUCTIONS

1 Mark the centre of the linen with lines of tacking thread and start stitching from this centre point following the equivalent point on the chart on page 84.

2 Work the cross stitching using two strands of cotton and the backstitching using a single strand.

3 Complete the cherub before moving on to the flowers and leaves. Finally, work the backstitched outlines.

MAKING UP

1 Place the opening of the card over the right side of the stitching and trim away any unstitched linen that extends beyond the edges of the card.

2 Attach strips of double-sided sticky tape on the inside of the card around the opening.

3 Place the card onto the fabric, making sure that the stitching lies centrally within the opening.

4 Turn the card to its wrong side and place strips of double-sided sticky tape around the edges of the left hand card flap.

5 Position the piece of polyester wadding over the back of the stitching, trimming if necessary, then press the left card flap down.

ADAPTATIONS AND VARIATIONS

1 For a completly different look to this design, change the colour of the linen to a dark one, such as navy blue or bottle green.

2 For a sparkly effect, substitute a metallic silver or gold thread for one of the strands of cotton in the cherub's hair or clothing.

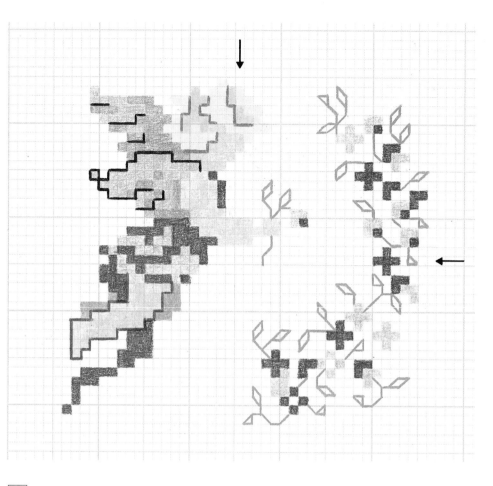

□ 745 very pale yellow

▨ 3325 pale dusty blue/776 rose pink

▨ 775 very pale dusty blue/819 very pale pink

▨ 758 very pale maroon

▨ 353 pale salmon pink

▨ 3770 pale creamy pink

▨ 743 orange yellow

▨ white

▨ 762 pale silver

— 564 pale silver green

— 415 silver

— 758 very pale maroon

— 743 orange yellow

Rocking Horse Greetings Card

This lovely card can be sent as it is, to be framed as a picture later, or could be framed initially and given as a gift. The frame could simply be fitted around the blue card or you could purchase a frame with an oval aperture, in which case the design would be mounted on a piece of stiff card before being placed in the frame.

Finished size of stitching:
14 × 9.5 cm (5½ × 3¾ in)

Finished size of card:
20 × 15 cm (8 × 6 in)

MATERIALS
White Aida, 18 count, size 19 × 15 cm
   (7½ × 6 in)

DMC STRANDED COTTON:

1 skein each of

- 798 blue
- 820 very dark blue
- 402 pale brown
- 959 aqua
- 726 pale gold
- 964 light aqua
- 921 orange brown
- 828 very pale sea blue

85

Tapestry needle, size 26
Blue card, aperture size 14×9.5 cm
   (5½×3¾ in), oval shaped
Double-sided sticky tape
2 oz polyester wadding, size 14×9.5 cm
   (5½×3¾ in)

STITCHING INSTRUCTIONS

1 Mark the centre of the Aida with lines of tacking thread and start stitching from this centre point following the equivalent point on the chart on page 88.

2 The stitching is worked in one strand of cotton, both for the cross stitch and the backstitch.

3 Complete the horse, reins and teddy but leave the outlining until the background stripes have been stitched.

4 Stitch the background stripes in cross stitch, then the work the outlining in back stitch. Finally, make a French knot for teddy's eye.

MAKING UP

1 Cut the piece of polyester wadding to the shape of the card aperture.

2 Follow the instructions for the Cherub Greetings Card to mount the embroidery in the card. Take care when positioning the card over the stitching that the background stripes are equally spaced from the ends of the card and that they are vertical.

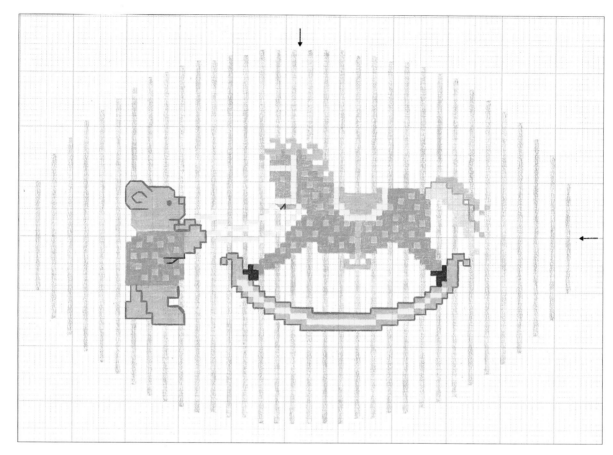

ADAPTATIONS AND VARIATIONS

1 Change the card and background stripe colour to co-ordinate with another colour scheme in the nursery.

2 If preferred, this design could be stitched on a much larger size of Aida to increase the overall picture size, for example on an 11 count fabric, the finished size would be 22.5 × 15 cm (9 × 6 in). Work using two strands of cotton.

3 Alternatively this design would be perfect as a door plaque. It could be personalised by including a name underneath the rocking horse using the alphabet on page 117.

798 blue
820 very dark blue
402 pale brown
959 aqua
726 pale gold
964 light aqua
— 921 orange brown
— 820 very dark blue
— 798 blue
828 very pale sea blue

Fairy Photograph Album Cover

Create this beautiful photograph album cover, to record those precious first few weeks of a baby's life, or as an extra special Christening Day gift.

This cover can be personalised by using the attractive illustrated alphabet. If, however, the baby's name is too long to fit the space, then stitch the initials only. Metallic thread has been used with the stranded cotton on the fairy's wings, to create a shimmering effect. A commercially bought album has been covered for this project, but alternatively one could be made using thick black paper and mount card for the cover.

Finished size of stitching:
16.5 × 19 cm (6½ × 7½ in)

Size of photograph album:
21 × 20 cm (8½ × 8 in)

MATERIALS

Blue Belfast linen, 32 count, size 52 × 28.5 cm (20¼ × 11 in)

DMC STRANDED COTTON:
1 skein each of

746 cream

3727 light antique pink

792 royal blue

793 light royal blue

B5200 snow white

820 very dark blue

950 pale mushroom

3747 palest violet

823 navy

3779 palest maroon

209 pale mauve

341 very pale violet

552 purple

955 pale aqua

954 pale green

722 dull orange

DMC METALLIC STRANDED THREAD:
1 skein of

silver

Tapestry needle, size 26
Photograph album, size 21 × 20 cm (8½ × 8 in)
2 oz polyester wadding, size 44 × 20 cm (17 × 8 in)
Fabric glue
Coloured paper or thin fabric for lining the inside of the album
Matching sewing thread
Ribbon, 6 mm (¼ in) wide, 1 m (39 in) long

STITCHING INSTRUCTIONS

1 All stitching is worked using one strand of cotton, except for the parts of the fairy's wings stitched in silver thread.

2 Mark the position of the frame to the centre panel with tacking stitches. The top and bottom edges are 9 cm (3½ in) from the edges of the linen and the right hand edge is 7 cm (2¾ in) from the right hand side of the linen. The panel is 12.5 cm (5 in) wide and 10.25 cm (4 in) deep.

3 Following the chart on page 92, stitch the frame to the centre panel within the stitched outline, using a straight stitch two threads long. Work the stitches in each hole of the linen so that they form a satin stitch effect.

4 Stitch the ribbon and bow at the top of the frame first, gradually working downwards so as to avoid rubbing existing work.

5 Next stitch the pram and fairy. For the parts of the wings stitched with silver thread use only one strand of silver together with one strand of cotton.

6 Work the flowers on either side of the bottom of the frame.

7 Using the alphabet at the end of the book, select the letters to be stitched. There is space for 62 stitches between the flowers at either side. Use a piece of graph paper to work out the positioning of your chosen letters, following the instructions on page 116. If the name is too long, work the initials only.

8 Finally stitch the silver stars, using one strand of thread. Use short lengths sufficient for one star at a time. This will avoid the tendency of the thread to shred.

MAKING UP

1 Remove the pages from the inside of the album, then place the piece of polyester wadding over the outside cover. Trim the sides of the wadding so that they are level with the edges of the album.

2 Place the stitched linen over the wadding, taking care to position the design centrally on the front cover.

3 Fold the excess linen to the wrong side and secure with glue. Remember to close the album when fitting the linen, in order to allow sufficient slack.

4 Cover the inside with the paper or fabric. If using paper, it can be glued into position. If using fabric, turn under all raw edges and slip stitch to the linen.

5 Re-assemble the album and thread through the ribbon, tying a bow on the front. If the ribbon is difficult to thread, use a large tapestry needle and push through.

ADAPTATIONS AND VARIATIONS

1 The centre panel of this design is perfect for using separately on a baby greetings card and could be stitched on 16 count Aida if preferred.

2 The attractive alphabet used here can be worked on numerous other projects, either as initials or as a full name. If a more substantial effect is required for the stitching, then use two strands of cotton instead of one.

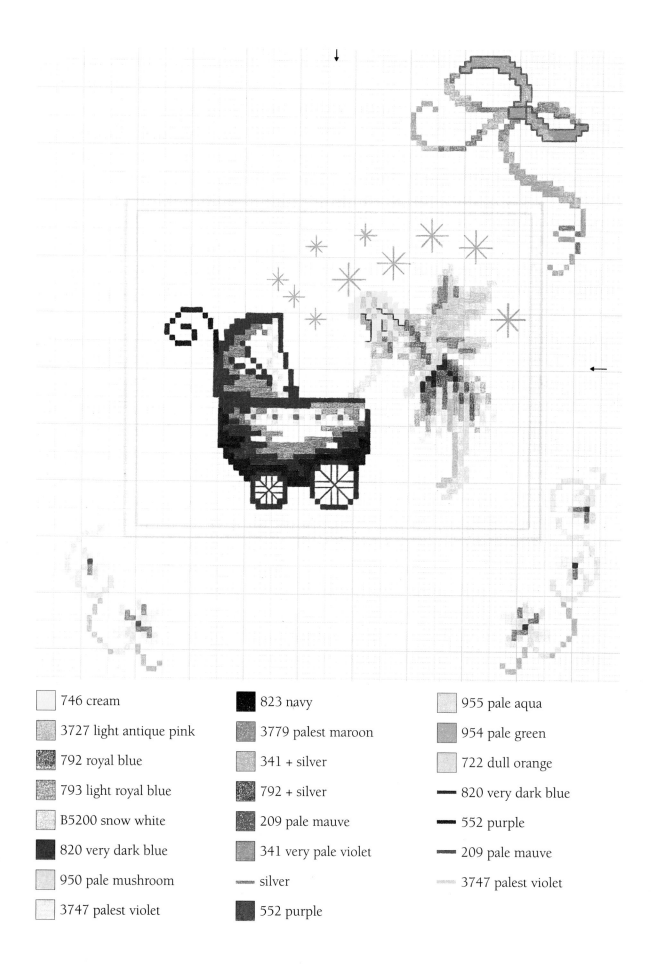

746 cream	823 navy	955 pale aqua
3727 light antique pink	3779 palest maroon	954 pale green
792 royal blue	341 + silver	722 dull orange
793 light royal blue	792 + silver	820 very dark blue
B5200 snow white	209 pale mauve	552 purple
820 very dark blue	341 very pale violet	209 pale mauve
950 pale mushroom	silver	3747 palest violet
3747 palest violet	552 purple	

Celebration Sampler

Stitching a sampler is a lovely way to celebrate the birth of a baby, or a first birthday. Band samplers made up of horizontal rows of letters, numbers and symbols are a traditional form of cross stitch embroidery dating from as far back as the 16th century. The particular symbols or motifs used often had a significant meaning and the sampler was usually personalised with the name or initials of the embroiderer. Examples of these classic samplers have survived and are preserved in museum collections. Yours, too, is likely to be treasured for many years to come.

Finished size of stitching:
8.5 × 17 cm
(3³⁄₈ × 6³⁄₄ in)

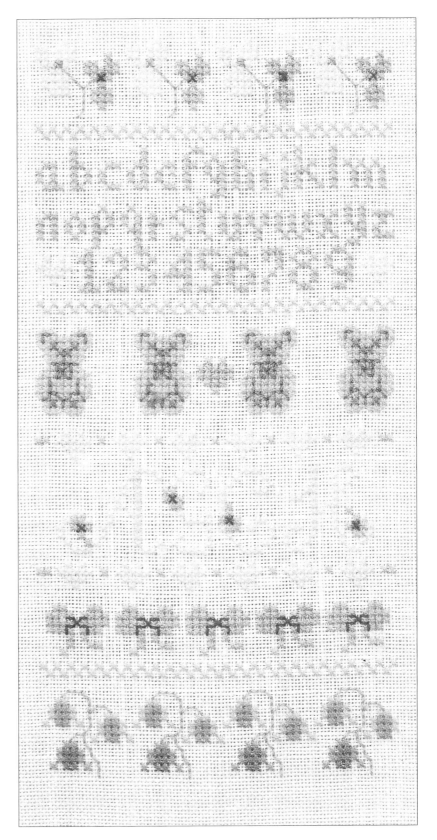

MATERIALS

White Belfast linen, 32 count, size 23×31 cm
    (9×12¼ in)

DMC FLOWER THREADS:

1 skein each of

- 2775 pale blue
- 2799 blue
- 2819 palest pink
- 2574 pale dusky pink
- 2899 bright pink
- 2504 pale green

Tapestry needle, size 26
2 oz polyester wadding, size 17×24.5 cm
    (6⅝×9¾ in)
Stiff white card for mounting the design, size
    17.5×25 cm (7×10 in)
Strong lacing thread, e.g. crochet cotton
Picture frame, size 17×24.5 cm (6⅝×9¾ in)

STITCHING INSTRUCTIONS

1 Place tacking stitches to mark the exact
position of the left and right sides of the
sampler. There are 51 squares of pattern in the
longest row. This will make the starting of each
row much easier and will act as a check when
finishing each row.

2 All the cross and the back stitching is
worked with a single strand of thread.

3 Following the chart on page 96, start
stitching the top row first, gradually
working down to the bottom. This will ensure
that the stitches once completed will not
become rubbed or soiled.

4 Take great care not to carry threads on the
back of the work from one area of stitching
to another, as these may show through onto the
right side.

MAKING UP

1 Remove the tacking stitches from the linen.
Place centrally over the polyester wadding,
right side up, then place centrally on top of the
mount card, again right side up.

2 Pin into the card along the four sides,
pulling the linen firmly.

3 On the wrong side, lace across from side to
side, and top to bottom, pulling the thread
tightly, following the instructions on page 115.
Fasten off the ends, and place the finished work
in the frame. Alternatively, the stitching can be
taken to a professional framer to be stretched
and mounted.

ADAPTATIONS AND VARIATIONS

1 The tiny motifs used on this sampler are
ideal for stitching on ribbons, using waste
canvas. These could be worked on ribbons to
attach to a bonnet, as bootee and mitten ties, or
on a ribbon to tie as a sash around a dress.

2 Another idea for using these motifs is to
stitch them on a padded photograph frame.
Each side of the frame could have a line of
different motifs, or the same motif could be
stitched in a different colour on each side.

3 The pink and blue flowers on the top and
bottom bands of this sampler would look
delightful if stitched alternately along an edge,
e.g. the hem of a dress or jacket.

- 2899 bright pink
- 2504 pale green
- 2799 blue
- 2775 pale blue
- 2799 blue
- 2819 palest pink
- 2574 pale dusky pink
- 2899 bright pink
- 2504 pale green

abcdefghijklm
nopqrstuvwxyz
1234567890

Rainbow Teddy Bear

Teddy bears must be one of the best loved toys, and you have only to ask how many adults still have their childhood bears to discover how long the affection lasts. Create an extra special bear with this delightful project. The stitching has been attached to a commercially bought bear but the bear could equally well be made from a purchased pattern using the Aida fabric.

Finished size of stitching:
approximately 9 × 12 cm (3½ × 4¾ in)

MATERIALS
White Aida, 18 count, size 17 × 14 cm
(6⅔ × 5½ in)

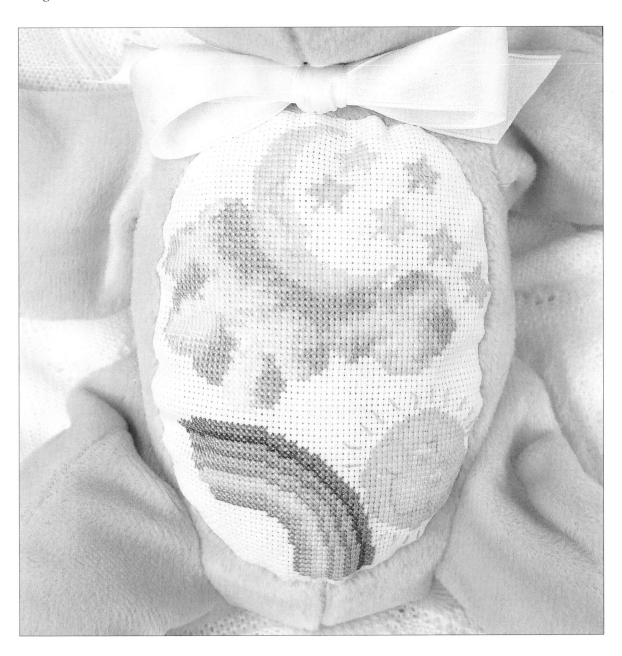

97

DMC STRANDED COTTON:

1 skein each of

727 pale yellow

3078 pale lemon

746 cream

827 pale sea blue

828 very pale sea blue

3756 very pale blue

B5200 snow white

972 bright orange

743 orange yellow

209 pale mauve

208 mauve

3755 dull blue

564 pale silver green

993 turquoise

3825 salmon pink

722 dull orange

Tapestry needle, size 26
Embroidery needle
Teddy bear, approximate tummy size
   15 × 11 cm (6 × 4¼ in)

STITCHING INSTRUCTIONS

1 Check the oval template on page 122 against the teddy bear you are using. If it needs to be smaller or larger, change the count size of the Aida fabric (see page 116). Use one strand of cotton throughout.

2 Following the chart on page 100, work all the cross stitches, starting from the centre and working outwards.

3 Finish by backstitching the outlines on the moon and sun.

MAKING UP

1 Using the oval template, trim the stitched Aida so that it extends just 1 cm (⅜ in) beyond the outline.

2 Snip the seam allowance and press under, so that the folded edge is a smooth curve.

3 Attach to the bear's tummy using blanket stitches and two strands of cotton in your chosen colour.

ADAPTATIONS AND VARIATIONS

Although this pattern has been designed as a single piece, it is made up of two groups of motifs which are as perfectly suited to being used separately as they are together. Place the sun and rainbow on Tee shirts, sun hats, etc., and the stars and moon on sleepsuits, pyjamas or a cot blanket.

▦ 727 pale yellow	▦ B5200 snow white	▦ 3755 dull blue
▢ 3078 pale lemon	— 972 bright orange	▦ 564 pale silver green
▢ 746 cream	— 743 orange yellow	▦ 993 turquoise
▦ 827 pale sea blue	▦ 743 orange yellow	▦ 3825 salmon pink
▢ 828 very pale sea blue	▦ 209 pale mauve	▦ 722 dull orange
▦ 3756 very pale blue	▦ 208 mauve	

Cheeky Clowns Number Picture

Create all the excitement of the Big Top with these playful circus clowns. This stunning picture will make a lively wall decoration for the nursery or playroom and is also designed to be an early learning aid. Each colourful clown has a number for his body and is dressed in striped trousers and a spotted shirt. As the numbers increase, so do the quantity of juggling balls but not all of them have stayed in the air.

Finished size of stitching:
50 × 30.5 cm (19¾ × 12 in)

Finished size of picture frame:
53.5 × 35cm (21 × 13½ in)

MATERIALS

White Belfast linen, 32 count, size 60 × 41 cm (24 × 16½ in)

DMC STRANDED COTTON:

1 skein each of

722 dull orange
819 very pale pink
210 light mauve
726 pale gold
727 pale yellow
954 pale green
3825 salmon pink
335 medium rose pink
white

972 bright orange
311 light navy
798 blue
911 bright green
921 orange brown
208 mauve

2 skeins each of

3716 pink
3755 dull blue

Tapestry needle, size 26
2 oz polyester wadding, size 50 × 31 cm (20 × 12 in)
Stiff white card for mounting the design, size 51 × 32 cm (20¼ × 12½ in)
Drawing pins
Strong thread for lacing
Large-eyed needle
Picture frame, size 50 × 31 cm (19⅝ × 12 in)

STITCHING INSTRUCTIONS

1 Place tacking stitches to mark the exact position of the four sides of the sampler. There are 305 stitches of pattern (i.e. 610 threads) across the width and 181 squares (362 threads) down each side. This will make the placing of the zig zag frame easier.

2 Stitch the zig zag lines first as follows, using two strands of thread over two threads,

following the chart on pages 105 to 107. Begin stitching the middle zig zag lines, then count blocks of 30 pairs (60 stitches) to position the vertical lines and mark each with a pin. Stitch the vertical lines. Finally stitch the top and bottom border lines.

3 Using two strands of thread and cross stitch, start working number 1 clown. Count to the middle of the block and complete the number itself before stitching the head, hands, feet and juggling balls.

4 Finish the clown by working as follows:
• the mouth, eyes, eyebrows, fingers, numbers, together with any shoe sole, hat and hair outlines using one strand of cotton in backstitch.
• the laces with two strands of cotton in backstitch.

5 When all the clowns have been completed, stitch the border of numbers and hats in cross stitch using two strands of cotton.

MAKING UP

1 Press the stitched linen on the wrong side and trim the edges to 7.5 cm (3 in) wide.

2 Place the linen centrally over the polyester wadding, right side up, then place

centrally on top of the mount card, again right side up. Using drawing pins, fix the linen and wadding along the top edge of the board, working from the centre outwards, then pin along the bottom edge and the sides. Fold the unworked linen to the back of the board, mitring the corners, following the instructions on page 115.

3 Using a long length of lacing thread, secure this at the centre top and lace from top to bottom and back up again. Start another thread at the centre top again and work out to the other side (see page 115).

4 Remove all the pins along the top and bottom edges and tighten up the lacing, fastening the threads securely at the ends.

5 Repeat this process with the side edges.

6 Place the finished work in the frame. Alternatively, the stitching can be taken to a professional framer to be stretched and mounted.

ADAPTATIONS AND VARIATIONS

1 If preferred the clowns could be stitched in one long line, instead of two, to make a frieze for the nursery wall. This would make a finished size of 99 × 18 cm (39 × 7 in).

2 The clowns could be stitched separately perhaps on a card for that special birthday.

3 A dark coloured linen fabric could be used to provide an interesting contrast.

3716 pink

722 dull orange

819 very pale pink

210 light mauve

726 pale gold

727 pale yellow

954 pale green

3755 dull blue

3825 salmon pink

335 medium rose pink

white

972 bright orange

335 medium rose pink

311 light navy

798 blue

911 bright green

921 orange brown

208 mauve

3755 dull blue

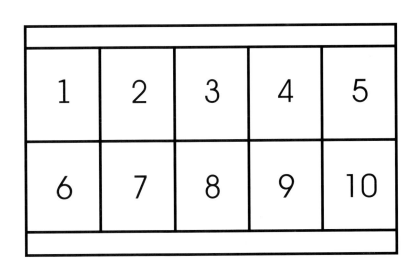

1	2	3	4	5
6	7	8	9	10

105

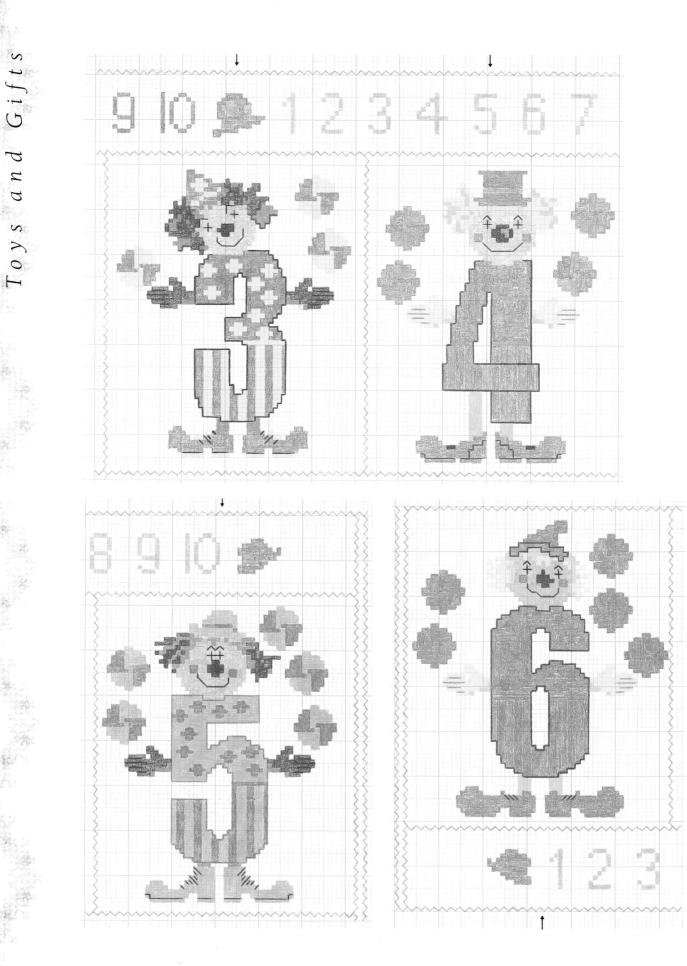

Chapter Four

Technicalities

Basic Techniques

Photograph Album Alphabet

Christening Gown Alphabet

Templates

DMC Shade Charts

Basic Techniques

CROSS STITCH FABRICS

Most cross stitch is worked on evenweave fabric, that is, fabric which has the same number of warp (vertical) threads as weft (horizontal) threads in a square area. These fabrics are graded according to the number of holes per inch, the higher the number, the finer the stitching. The grading is called the "count" of the fabric.

Aida is one of the most popular evenweave fabrics, especially for beginners, as it woven in such a way as to present distinctive squares. These are easy both to see and to stitch. Aida is available in a wide range of colours from white through all the colours of the rainbow to black. The sizes start at 8 holes per inch (8 count), going up to the finest of 18 holes per inch, with different fibre contents ranging from cotton to rayon and linen.

There are several other fabrics on which cross stitching is worked over every thread e.g. Hardanger and Oslo. However, there is a wide range of linens and other evenweave fabrics on which stitches are worked over two threads. At first it may seem a little difficult to count the threads and to position the needle, especially after using Aida. However, with practice it becomes much easier and after a while quite instinctive. Many of the projects here are stitched on 32 count Belfast linen, which has produced a very traditional look.

PREPARING THE FABRIC

Once the evenweave fabric has been cut to size, it is advisable to finish the raw edges, so as to avoid fraying whilst stitching. There are various different ways of achieving this and most stitchers have a personal favourite. Cutting with pinking shears is certainly the quickest and is ideal for small projects but would probably still result in fraying on larger pieces of work. Oversewing by hand, machine zig-zag stitch, bias binding, or turning a hem are all be suitable. Masking tape can be used but it sometimes pulls out fabric threads when it is removed.

WORKING WHOLE CROSS STITCHES

There are two methods for working cross stitch.

Method 1
Complete each cross stitch before moving onto the next (diagram 1).

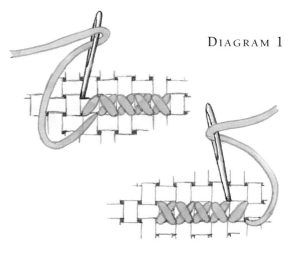

DIAGRAM 1

Method 2
Work across the row stitching one half of each cross, before working in the opposite direction to complete the stitches (diagram 2).

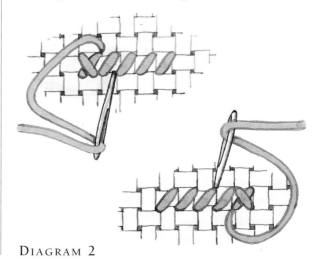

DIAGRAM 2

Either of these methods can be used to work vertical lines of stitches (diagrams 3 and 4).

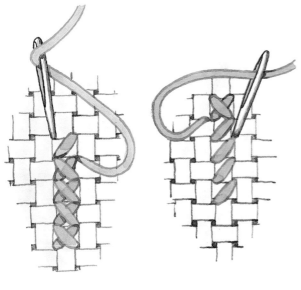

half stitch completed in one movement (diagram 6).

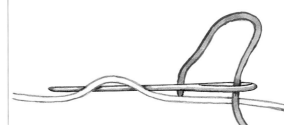

DIAGRAM 3   DIAGRAM 4

You will notice that in the stitches illustrated, the second half of the cross is always made in the same direction. This is important if the piece of stitching is to look neat and regular. However, it doesn't make any difference whether these upper stitches lie from right to left or left to right.

The best way of working a cross stitch is to bring the needle entirely down through the fabric, before bringing it back up again (diagram 5). This two-step method for one half of the cross gives a more even tension to the work than if the fabric is crumpled up and the

DIAGRAM 6

WORKING THREE-QUARTER
STITCHES
These are used to give a less stepped and more realistic shape to a motif. They consist of one full length diagonal and one half length. On the charts they are identified by only half the square being coloured in.

You will see these have been used on the Celebration Sampler and the Rocking Horse Greetings Card. As the sampler was stitched on linen, the half stitches use the existing hole in the centre of the square of threads used by each cross stitch. However, to make the half stitches on the Aida of the Greetings Card, the needle has to pierce through the threads in the exact central position.

Diagrams 7 and 8 show how these stitches are worked. If there is an outline backstitch also

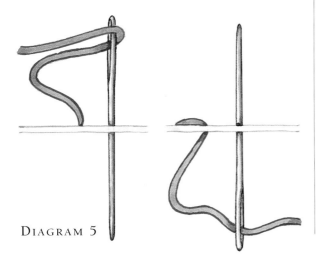

DIAGRAM 5

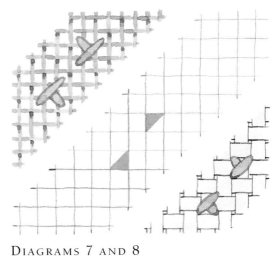

DIAGRAMS 7 AND 8

being worked in exactly the same position as the long part of the three-quarter stitch, then this part of the stitch is best omitted (diagram 9).

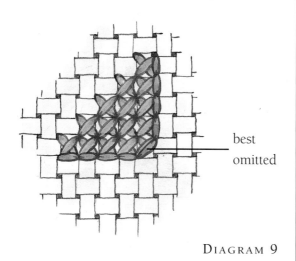

best
omitted

DIAGRAM 9

BACK STITCH

This forms a continuous line and is used to give extra definition to the shape of a motif, or to separate two areas of stitching. Diagram 10 shows how the needle comes up at 1, down at 2, up at 3, down at 4, etc. It can be worked in a horizontal, vertical or diagonal direction.

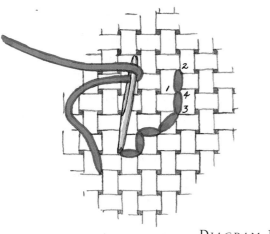

DIAGRAM 10

FRENCH KNOTS

These are used to give additional detail to an area of stitching, as well as a textured surface. The size of the knot depends on the thickness of thread used and the number of twists made. Bring the thread up at the required position and

hold this with the left thumb, whilst twisting the needle twice around the thread. Insert the needle back into the fabric, close to the original position. Pull through gently to the back and finish off (diagram 11).

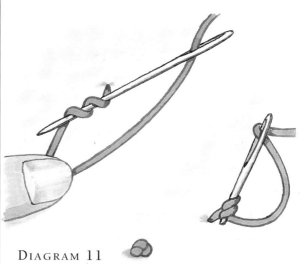

DIAGRAM 11

WORKING FROM CHARTS AND KEYS

Each square on the chart represents one cross stitch, worked over either one square of Aida or two threads of linen. A partially coloured square represents a three-quarter stitch.

Any backstitching that has been used on a design is identified by the bold, different coloured straight lines around or through the coloured blocks. The key gives the colour numbers of the threads to be used. All the colours shown are as near as possible to the real thread colours but where several close shades have been used in the stitching, the differences have been exaggerated on the chart, or in some cases changed altogether (for example, for white threads), to help you distinguish between the shades.

DMC stranded cottons and flower threads have been used throughout this book. If other brands of threads are used, consult the manufacturer's conversion charts. However, it is worth checking that the recommended thread is a close substitute colour.

USING A HOOP OR FRAME

It is not essential to frame a piece of work in progress but a more even tension is usually achieved if one is used. For small pieces of work, an embroidery hoop is ideal. However, ensure that it is large enough to frame the entire piece of stitching, as it is not advisable to squash any stitching between the two rings.

Attach the hoop by laying the fabric over the inner ring, right side up, then press the outer ring in place, making sure that the warp and weft threads of the fabric are straight. Tighten up the outer ring, so that the fabric remains taut while stitching. It is a good idea to bind the inner ring with opened out bias binding or strips of cotton fabric. This will give the ring a better grip as well as making it less liable to mark the fabric whilst in use. It is advisable to remove the ring between stitching sessions, to prevent the fabric becoming stretched and distorted.

If the piece of Aida or linen being used is too small to fit into the hoop, extend this by sewing on a piece of cotton fabric to the wrong side, then cut away the cotton at the back of the evenweave (diagram 12).

Slate frames, where the top and bottom edges of the fabric are attached to rollers, are ideal for larger projects. Once the tension is achieved by tightening up the roller bars, the fabric should be laced over the side bars. These slate frames can be hand-held or floor standing. The main advantage of a floor frame is that both hands are released for stitching. One hand can be positioned below the work and one above, which speeds up the stitching process.

NEEDLES

Size 24 or 26 tapestry needles are used for most Aida and evenweave fabrics. The blunt ends of these needles will not split the fabric threads while stitching. This correct size of needle will ensure that it slides easily through the holes, without pushing the fabric threads apart. If this does happen the finished stitching tends to have a perforated look.

THREADS

Stranded cotton or floss has been used for the majority of the projects. This is divisible into six strands. Cut into lengths of approximately 45 cm (18 in), then separate into single strands. If more than one strand is being used, re-combine the required number, which will give a flatter, fuller look to the stitching.

"Flower Threads" have been used for a small number of the projects. This is a non-divisible, matt thread with a thickness approximately equivalent to two strands of floss.

Metallic thread has been included in the "Fairy Photograph Album Cover" and the "Cherub Greetings Card" projects. As this frays easily when being stitched, it is essential to use short lengths. This type of thread is also notoriously bad for slipping in the needle. It may help to tie a single knot at the end of the needle eye. Alternatively, try placing your thumb over the stitches already completed to hold them in place, while working the next ones.

It may be helpful to use a thread organiser for any project where a large number of colours is used. This is a strip of card with holes punched down one side. Either knot small pieces of each

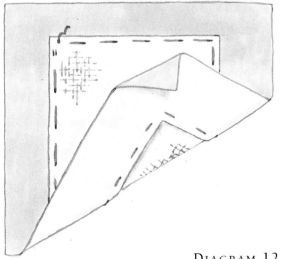

DIAGRAM 12

colour of thread in the holes and label them with the colour number, or cut all the thread into 45 cm (18 in) lengths and knot into the holes before starting the project.

If threads have been bent or folded for a long time, it is better to straighten them before stitching. This is easily done by separating into individual strands and moistening them with a damp sponge. Once dry, the threads will be ready to use.

When stitching, complete one colour area at a time. Avoid carrying threads across more than a few stitches on the reverse side, as this can cause puckering of the fabric. More importantly, strands of thread, especially dark ones, can show through to the right side of the fabric.

STARTING TO STITCH

Method 1
Leave a short length of thread on the wrong side, then make sure this is worked over with the first few stitches.

Method 2
This method is only suitable for when you are using two strands of cotton for the stitching. Cut a single strand of thread twice as long as usual, fold in half and thread the cut ends through the needle. Stitch the first part of the first stitch, bringing the needle up from the wrong side, then down again through the loop on the back of the fabric (diagram 13). This

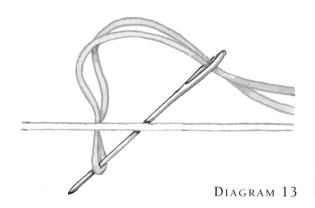

DIAGRAM 13

method is perfect for areas of stitching where the reverse side may be seen, as it eliminates the need to stitch over the thread end.

It is usually best to start stitching in the centre of the design, so that the finished stitching will be surrounded by an even amount of fabric. This is especially important when the size of the design has been changed, or when a repeat pattern needs to be centralised. However, on a large project it can be better to start stitching at the top and to work downwards, so that the stitching remains clean and unrubbed.

To find the centre of the piece of fabric, fold in half lengthways and mark the crease with a line of tacking stitches, through a line of holes. Use contrasting thread for this, then repeat widthways.

FINISHING STITCHING
Run the needle and thread through the last few stitches on the wrong side of the work, then snip off the end.

USING WASTE CANVAS
Waste canvas provides a temporary, countable grid, which is removed once stitching is completed. It is ideal for use on non-woven fabrics, such as felt, or those with a non-definable weave, such as towelling.

Take care to position the needle through the centre of the holes in the canvas, as these are quite large and the stitches could be formed in different sizes. If the points of the cross stitches always meet, then an even finish will result.

Backstitching on waste canvas is normally worked before the canvas is removed. However, it is possible to do this afterwards, which does have the advantage that the stitches can be positioned more precisely. It is a good idea to experiment to find which method you prefer before embarking on a project.

If you are making up the item in the project, rather than working on a purchased piece, it is much easier to work the cross stitching before the piece is assembled. This is particularly relevant where the stitching space is confined, or where stitching would otherwise be worked through several layers of fabric.

It is a good idea to use a close machine zig-zag stitch or binding on the cut edges of the waste canvas, so that these do not snag the fabric of the item being stitched.

Tack the waste canvas over the area to be stitched, taking care not to stretch the stitching surface. The tacking stitches should radiate out from the centre as well as forming a border round the edges, to ensure that the canvas is held securely.

Use a sharp-pointed needle instead of the usual blunt tapestry one, so that it slips easily through the stitching fabric. However, take care not to pierce the canvas threads. Work all stitches over a pair of threads.

Once the stitching is completed, remove the tacking stitches from the waste canvas, then soften by laying over a dampened towel for a short while. Cut away any excess canvas, but do not cut right up to the stitching, as you will need 2 cm (¾ in) to hold when pulling the threads.

Try to remove the warp (vertical) threads first, as these are slightly stronger and will pull without breaking. Take great care with this process so as not to damage the fabric underneath. If any canvas threads are particularly stubborn, use tweezers to remove them.

LACING WORK FOR FRAMING
Use acid-free mount board if possible, cut to the same size as the frame; 2 oz polyester wadding is also recommended as a backing to the stitching, as this gives a slightly raised effect to the piece of work.

Lay the stitched fabric over the wadding, on top of the card, matching centre points.

Push pins through the fabric into the board, working from the centre outwards on each side, pulling the fabric gently so that there is equal tautness all over.

Fold the unworked fabric to the back of the board, mitreing the corners, as shown in diagram 14. This will reduce excess bulk of fabric.

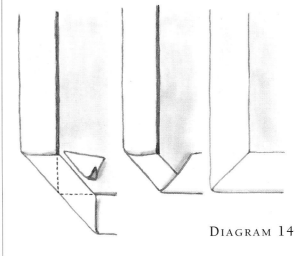

DIAGRAM 14

On the reverse side, using a long length of strong thread and a large eyed needle, lace the two opposite sides together from top to bottom. Use an "under and over" movement for this, starting at either the right or left side. Stop in the centre, leaving the end to be tightened up later.

Repeat this lacing from the other side to the centre, then remove any slack before tying a knot with the two ends.

The lacing should now be repeated on the sides (diagram 15).

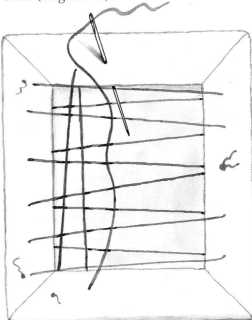

DIAGRAM 15

FRAMING

Whether to include glass or not over your piece of stitching must be a personal choice. It protects the work from dust, the biggest enemy to any fabric, and also from direct sunlight. However, the glass does tend to camouflage the stitching, so that the texture and detail are not as easily seen.

WASHING

If the piece of work is completed relatively quickly, is covered up when not being worked on and hands are always clean, then it should not need to be washed. However, some stitchers prefer always to wash their work to give it a fresh look. Immerse the stitched piece in lukewarm water and mild soap suds or needlework shampoo. Either leave to dry a little first, or iron straightaway. Place the work face down on an ironing board padded with a thick, clean towel. Cover with a clean cloth, then press carefully until dry. The thickness of the towel will prevent the stitching from being flattened.

POSITIONING LETTERING

The "Fairy Photograph Album Cover" has a space for you to insert a name or initials of your choice. To do this, count the number of stitches needed for the required letters, adding one space between each letter. Count the number of spaces available, then subtract the number needed for the letters. The remaining spaces can then be equally divided among the letters or shared between the two ends. The spacing between letters should be a minimum of one, but should not be too large, or the overall effect becomes disjointed.

Once the layout is decided, draw out the letters onto graph paper ready for stitching.

CHANGING THE SIZE OF A DESIGN

It is extremely useful to be able to change the dimensions of a design, especially as your bought items for these projects may vary slightly in style or size.

Simply use a fabric with a different count. A higher count, e.g. 10 to 14, will give a smaller size and a lower count, e.g. 14 to 10, will result in a larger design.

To work out the changed size, count the total number of squares in the longest horizontal line and in the longest vertical line on the chart to be stitched and divide each by the number of holes per inch on the fabric to be used. For example, if the design is 32 squares high and 22 squares wide

• using 11 count fabric, the stitching will be 3 in high and 2 in wide (7.5 × 5 cm).

• using 32 count linen (stitched over 2 threads, i.e. 16 count), the stitching will be 2 in high and 1⅜ in wide (5 × 3.5 cm).

Photograph Album Alphabet

3747 palest violet   341 very pale violet

117

Christening Gown Alphabet

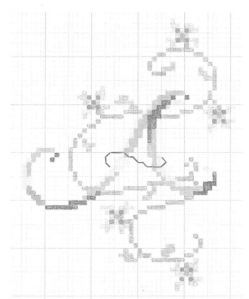

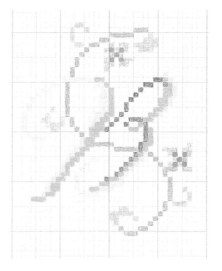

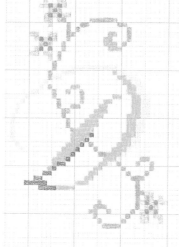

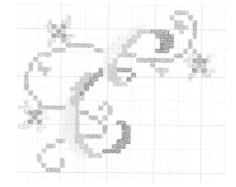

966 pale fern green

564 pale silver green

827 pale sea blue

775 very pale dusty blue

352 salmon pink

754 very pale salmon pink

948 creamy pink

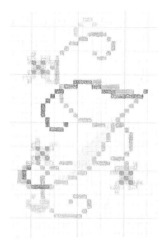

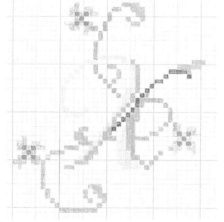
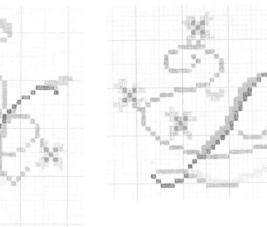

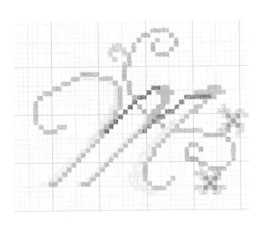
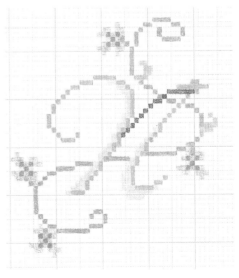

966 pale
fern green

564 pale
silver green

827 pale sea
blue

775 very
pale dusty blue

352 salmon
pink

754 very pale
salmon pink

948 creamy
pink

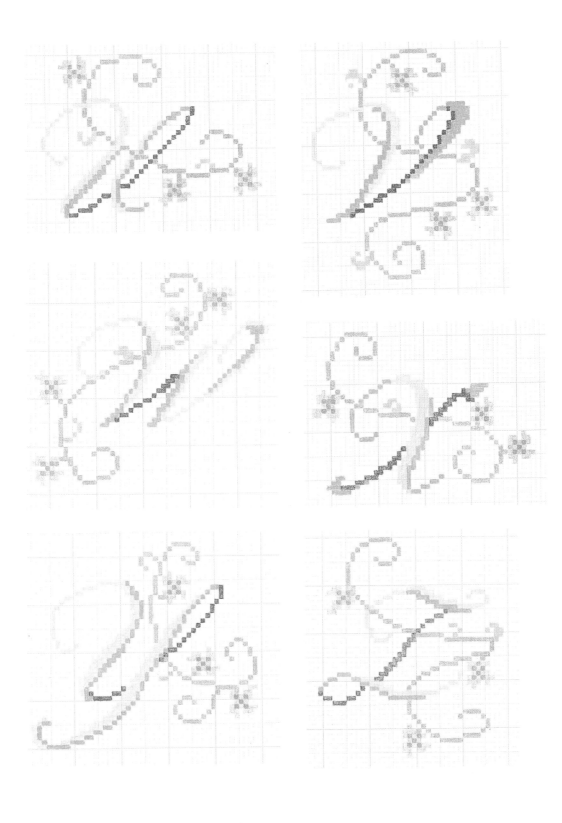

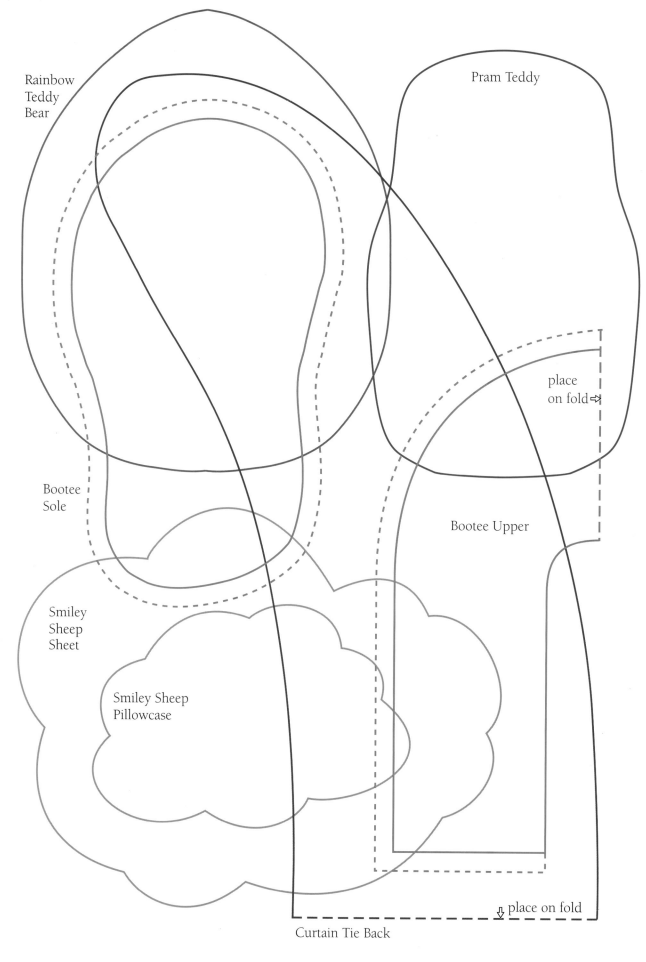

Rainbow
Teddy
Bear

Pram Teddy

place
on fold ⇨

Bootee
Sole

Bootee Upper

Smiley
Sheep
Sheet

Smiley Sheep
Pillowcase

⇩ place on fold

Curtain Tie Back

DMC Stranded Cotton

Colour	Key	Colour	Key	Colour	Key	Colour	Key	Colour	Key	Colour	Key	Colour	Key	Colour	Key	Colour	Key	Colour	Key
ecrut	22	211	6	400	19	563	11	727	17	813	8	910	11	971	18	3347	12	3773	20
blanc	22	221	5	402	19	564	11	729	16	814	2	911	11	972	18	3348	12	3774	20
B5200	22	223	5	407	20	580	14	730	14	815	2	912	11	973	18	3350	3	3776	19
48	24	224	5	413	23	581	14	731	14	816	2	913	11	975	19	3354	3	3777	20
51	26	225	5	414	23	597	9	732	14	817	1	915	4	976	19	3362	13	3778	20
52	24	300	19	415	23	598	9	733	14	818	3	917	4	977	19	3363	13	3779	20
53	26	301	19	420	16	600	4	734	14	819	3	918	19	986	12	3364	13	3781	22
57	24	304	2	422	16	601	4	738	21	820	7	919	19	987	12	3371	21	3782	22
61	26	307	17	433	21	602	4	739	21	822	22	920	19	988	12	3607	4	3787	22
62	24	309	3	434	21	603	4	740	17	823	8	921	19	989	12	3608	4	3790	22
67	25	310	23	435	21	604	4	741	17	824	8	922	19	991	10	3609	4	3799	23
69	26	311	8	436	21	605	4	742	17	825	8	924	10	992	10	3685	3	3801	2
75	24	312	8	437	21	606	18	743	17	826	8	926	10	993	10	3687	3	3802	5
90	26	315	5	444	17	608	18	744	17	827	8	927	10	995	9	3688	3	3803	3
91	25	316	5	445	17	610	15	745	17	828	8	928	10	996	9	3689	3	3804	4
92	25	317	23	451	23	611	15	746	16	829	15	930	7	3011	15	3705	2	3805	4
93	25	318	23	452	23	612	15	747	9	830	15	931	7	3012	15	3706	2	3806	4
94	26	319	12	453	23	613	15	754	1	831	15	932	7	3013	15	3708	2	3807	7
95	24	320	12	469	13	632	20	758	20	832	15	934	13	3021	22	3712	1	3808	9
99	24	321	2	470	13	640	22	760	1	833	15	935	13	3022	22	3713	1	3809	9
101	25	322	8	471	13	642	22	761	1	834	15	936	13	3023	22	3716	2	3810	9
102	24	326	3	472	13	644	22	762	23	838	21	937	13	3024	22	3721	5	3811	9
103	25	327	6	498	2	645	23	772	12	839	21	938	21	3031	22	3722	5	3812	10
104	26	333	6	500	11	646	23	775	8	840	21	939	8	3032	22	3726	5	3813	11
105	26	334	8	501	11	647	23	776	3	841	21	943	10	3033	22	3727	5	3814	10
106	26	335	3	502	11	648	23	778	5	842	21	945	20	3041	5	3731	3	3815	10
107	24	336	8	503	11	666	2	780	16	844	23	946	18	3042	5	3733	3	3816	10
108	26	340	6	504	11	676	16	781	16	869	16	947	18	3045	16	3740	5	3817	10
111	26	341	6	517	9	677	16	782	16	890	12	948	1	3046	16	3743	5	3818	11
112	24	347	1	518	9	680	16	783	16	891	1	950	20	3047	16	3746	6	3819	14
113	25	349	1	519	9	699	14	791	7	892	1	951	20	3051	13	3747	6	3820	17
114	25	350	1	520	13	700	14	792	7	893	1	954	11	3052	13	3750	7	3821	17
115	24	351	1	522	13	701	14	793	7	894	1	955	11	3053	13	3752	7	3822	17
116	24	352	1	523	13	702	14	794	7	895	12	956	2	3064	20	3753	7	3823	17
121	25	353	1	524	13	703	14	796	7	898	21	957	2	3072	23	3755	8	3824	18
122	25	355	20	535	23	704	14	797	7	899	3	958	10	3078	17	3756	8	3825	18
123	25	356	20	543	21	712	21	798	7	900	18	959	10	3325	8	3760	9	3826	19
124	25	367	12	550	6	718	4	799	7	902	5	961	2	3326	3	3761	9	3827	19
125	25	368	12	552	6	720	18	800	7	904	14	962	2	3328	1	3765	9	3828	16
126	24	369	12	553	6	721	18	801	21	905	14	963	2	3340	18	3766	9	3829	16
208	6	370	15	554	6	722	18	806	9	906	14	964	10	3341	18	3768	10	3830	20
209	6	371	15	561	11	725	17	807	9	907	14	966	12	3345	12	3770	20		
210	6	372	15	562	11	726	17	809	7	909	11	970	18	3346	12	3772	20		

Key to colour numbers

1	2	3	4	5	6
3713	963	819	3806	225	554
761	3716	818	3805	224	553
760	962	776	3804	223	552
3712	961	3326	605	3722	550
3328	957	899	604	3721	211
347	956	335	603	221	210
948	3708	309	602	778	209
754	3706	326	601	3727	208
353	3705	3354	600	316	327
352	3801	3733	3609	3726	3747
351	666	3731	3608	315	341
350	321	3350	3607	3802	340
349	304	3689	718	902	3746
817	498	3688	917	3743	333
894	816	3687	915	3042	
893	815	3803		3041	
892	814	3685		3740	
891					

7	8	9	10	11	12
794	3756	3761	964	504	966
793	775	519	959	3813	369
3807	3325	518	958	503	368
792	3755	3760	3812	502	320
791	334	517	943	501	367
800	322	996	993	500	319
809	312	995	992	564	890
799	311	747	3814	563	989
798	336	3766	991	562	988
797	823	807	928	561	987
796	939	806	927	955	986
820	828	3765	926	954	772
3753	827	3811	3728	913	3348
3752	813	598	924	912	3347
932	826	597	3817	911	3346
931	825	3810	3816	910	3345
930	824	3809	3815	909	895
3750		3808		3818	

13	14	15	16	17	18
524	704	3013	3047	3822	973
523	703	3012	3046	3821	972
522	702	3011	3045	3820	971
520	701	372	422	445	970
3053	700	371	3828	307	947
3052	699	370	420	444	946
3051	907	834	869	3078	900
3364	906	833	783	727	608
3363	905	832	782	726	606
3362	904	831	781	725	3824
472	3819	830	780	3823	3341
471	581	829	746	745	3340
470	580	613	677	744	3825
469	734	612	676	743	722
937	733	611	729	742	721
936	732	610	680	741	720
935	731		3829	740	
934	730				

19	20	21	22	23
922	3770	712	B5200	453
921	951	739	BLANC	452
920	945	738	ECRUT	451
919	3774	437	3024	535
918	950	436	3023	3072
402	3773	435	3022	648
3776	3064	434	3787	647
301	407	433	3021	646
400	3772	801	822	645
300	632	898	644	844
3827	3779	938	642	762
977	758	3371	640	415
976	3778	543	3790	318
3826	356	842	3033	414
975	3830	841	3782	317
	355	840	3032	413
	3777	839	3781	3799
		838	3031	310

white	10	2325	4	2405	9	2574	1	2724	2	2776	1	2833	7	2924	5
ECRU	10	2326	1	2407	9	2579	6	2725	7	2778	2	2836	7	2926	5
2209	3	2327	2	2413	10	2590	4	2726	7	2782	7	2839	9	2927	5
2210	3	2329	2	2414	10	2592	4	2727	7	2783	7	2840	9	2928	5
2211	3	2333	3	2415	10	2594	4	2728	2	2788	6	2841	9	2929	4
2221	2	2337	4	2433	10	2595	5	2730	7	2797	3	2842	9	2930	4
2222	2	2346	1	2434	10	2597	5	2732	7	2798	3	2890	6	2931	4
2223	2	2349	8	2436	10	2599	5	2734	7	2799	3	2898	10	2932	4
2225	2	2350	8	2446	7	2608	2	2738	10	2800	3	2899	1	2933	4
2241	9	2351	8	2469	5	2609	10	2740	8	2801	10	2902	1	2937	5
2280	9	2352	8	2471	5	2610	7	2742	8	2814	1	2905	6	2938	9
2303	8	2353	8	2472	5	2611	7	2743	8	2815	1	2906	6	2946	8
2304	1	2354	8	2497	2	2613	7	2745	8	2818	1	2907	6	2947	8
2309	1	2356	8	2499	6	2632	9	2748	8	2819	1	2909	5	2948	9
2310	10	2358	3	2500	6	2640	10	2754	8	2820	3	2911	5	2950	9
2312	4	2359	3	2501	6	2642	10	2758	8	2823	3	2912	5	2952	5
2315	2	2369	6	2502	6	2644	10	2759	8	2824	4	2916	2	2956	5
2316	2	2371	10	2503	6	2666	1	2760	2	2825	4	2917	2	2958	5
2318	10	2394	3	2504	6	2673	6	2761	2	2826	4	2918	9	2986	6
2319	6	2395	3	2531	3	2706	1	2766	7	2827	4	2919	9		
2320	6	2396	3	2532	3	2708	1	2768	5	2828	4	2921	9		
2321	1	2397	3	570	1	2715	6	2773	9	2829	7	2922	9		
2322	4	2400	7	2572	1	2719	2	2775	4	2831	7	2923	9		

Key to colour numbers

1	2	3	4	5
2708	2761	2396	2775	2599
2706	2760	2397	2325	2597
2666	2329	2395	2322	2595
2321	2327	2394	2312	2928
2304	2225	2211	2337	2927
2346	2223	2210	2828	2926
2815	2222	2209	2827	2768
2819	2221	2532	2826	2924
2818	2778	2531	2825	2952
2776	2728	2358	2824	2956
2899	2316	2359	2594	2958
2309	2724	2333	2592	2912
2326	2315	2800	2590	2911
2574	2497	2799	2933	2909
2572	2608	2798	2932	2472
2570	2719	2797	2931	2471
2814	2917	2820	2930	2469
2902	2916	2823	2929	2937

6	7	8	9	10
2504	2446	2745	2923	ECRU
2503	2734	2743	2922	2738
2502	2732	2748	2921	2436
2501	2730	2742	2919	2434
2500	2833	2740	2918	2433
2499	2831	2947	2950	2801
2715	2829	2946	2407	2898
2369	2613	2754	2405	2371
2320	2611	2353	2632	2644
2319	2610	2352	2948	2642
2890	2727	2351	2842	2640
2788	2726	2350	2841	2609
2907	2725	2349	2840	2415
2906	2783	2759	2839	2318
2905	2782	2758	2938	2414
2986	2766	2356	2280	2413
2579	2836	2303	2773	2310
2673	2400	2354	2241	WHITE

Index

SUPPLIERS

DMC Creative World Ltd
Pullman Road, Wigston, Leicestershire
LE18 2DY

Macleod Craft Marketing
West Yonderton, Warlock Road,
Bridge of Weir, Renfrewshire PA11 3SR

Anna French Ltd
108 Shakespeare Road, London SE24 0QW

The Pier
200 Tottenham Court Road, London W1

ACKNOWLEDGEMENTS

The author and publishers would like to thank the following
people and companies for supplying materials and for help
with the stitching and making up of the projects:

DMC for supplying all the threads, Zweigart fabrics and
canvases;
Anna French for the curtain fabric;
Macleod Craft Marketing for the hooded towel;
The Pier for supplying props for photography;
Eileen Adams, Beryl Miller, June Misom, Ann Phillips and
Vivien Staunton for their stitching.